POLITICAL PHILOSOPHY A–Z

Volumes available in the Philosophy A–Z Series

Forthcoming volumes

Political Philosophy A–Z

Jon Pike

Edinburgh University Press

© Jon Pike, 2007

Edinburgh University Press Ltd
22 George Square, Edinburgh

Typeset in 10.5/13 Sabon by
Servis Filmsetting Ltd, Manchester, and
printed and bound in Great Britain by
Antony Rowe Ltd, Chippenham, Wilts

A CIP record for this book is
available from the British Library

ISBN 978 0 7486 2269 6 (hardback)
ISBN 978 0 7486 2270 2 (paperback)

The right of Jon Pike
to be identified as author of this work
has been asserted in accordance with
the Copyright, Designs and Patents Act 1988.

Contents

Series Editor's Preface

Political philosophy is one of those areas of philosophy that have a foot in theory and one also firmly placed in the practice of social life. Although much of the discipline can be technical and complex, so is living in society. Understanding the principles that lie behind society and how it operates is clearly not going to be a simple matter, and philosophy deepens the issue even further by considering the possibility of a whole range of explanations for political phenomena. In this context theoretical questions such as who has the right to govern, what is democracy and how can justice be made the principle of government are raised as part and parcel of ordinary political debate. We may think we know how to respond to these questions, yet that is often because we are operating firmly within a particular political context and do not pay sufficient attention to the range of different theories and viewpoints that are available to us. Before we can understand the nature of anything in politics we need to have a grasp of the wide range of contexts in which political ideas function, and how they are used differently depending upon the ideological framework of the participants. In this book Jon Pike has explored a variety of the most significant concepts in political philosophy and the intention is to provide readers with a helpful range of explanations of the discipline's basic ideas and issues.

Oliver Leaman

Introduction

Political philosophy is one of the most widely taught branches of philosophy, perhaps because it seems to be of direct and immediate importance. Because it is political, political philosophy doesn't leave things just where they are (in the way that, for example, linguistic analysis does). At university level, philosophy is often studied alongside other disciplines, rather than as a single honours course – and here political philosophy seems to fit well, from the traditional Oxford model of Politics, Philosophy and Economics to joint honours degrees around the world. This may make it seem that political philosophy is a discipline with porous borders: on the one hand to the social sciences and on the other to other parts of the discipline of philosophy as a whole. This is not a wholly misleading impression, which makes writing a book which aims at some degree of comprehensiveness virtually impossible: just where does the subject stop?

In some respects this is an easy question to answer. In terms of historical figures, there is a measure of agreement about the canon (and truth by agreement is all that is required here). Plato and Aristotle kick things off, and the key figures – Hobbes, Locke, Rousseau, Mill and Marx, up to the twentieth century, are fairly obvious. It is there that things get complicated and contentious. What is more, this concern is perhaps exacerbated by the development of the subject in the last 30 or so years, since the publication of John Rawls's *Theory of Justice*. In the wake of the protests against the

Vietnam War on US campuses, a new intellectual phenomenon emerged of philosophical engagement with political affairs in a rigorous, radical and (usually) accessible way, exemplified by the journal *Philosophy and Public Affairs*, which joined *Ethics* as the key spaces for new work in the discipline. Together these mark out the terrain and the most porous border of all, between political philosophy on one side and applied ethics and moral philosophy on the other. In what follows, this border is not seriously policed.

Two other territorial disputes deserve comment: one is between political philosophy and 'Political Theory' and the other, within philosophy itself, is between what have come to be called – regrettably – analytical and continental approaches. These two distinctions sometimes seem to join hands: people who call themselves political theorists are often more open to 'continental' approaches than people who call themselves political philosophers. The general approach taken here is that the lines between political philosophy on the one hand and political theory, critical theory and applied philosophy on the other are not always clear, but the core concerns of political philosophy can be specified. It is a largely normative enterprise and concerned with relations between individuals, groups and the state. Its normativity – its concern with how we ought to live, how we ought to construct political institutions, laws and rules, and the nature of our relation to those institutions laws and rules – is generally unabashed. Political philosophers don't mind telling people what they ought, in the abstract, to do. Nonetheless, despite its being a normative enterprise, political philosophy does, to the consternation of some students, leave much more in place than they might have expected. Political philosophers are not averse to outlining principles of justice, but these are generally abstract principles of justice couched in hypothetical terms, depending for their application on masses of empirical and social information, which is often unavailable in practice and even in principle. For example, endorsement of the difference principle does not map easily onto a particular position in political debates over taxation. Political philosophy is often played out at a level of abstraction that is remote from actual policy. Much political theory closes that gap. For example, political theory provides simplified models of real-world political change – what might be called ideal descriptive theory. Theories of the development of class-based social democratic parties which conform to Michels's iron law of oligarchy would fall into this category. Social scientific and psychological generalisations that constitute ideal descriptive theory are often assumed in political philosophy as it is conceived here, but they constitute a different realm and there is a legitimate academic division of labour between political philosophers and political theorists, thought of course there is much cross-fertilisation. This is particularly true in some of the freshest areas of the discipline such as discussions of deliberative democracy and multiculturalism.

The question of the so-called 'analytic/continental' divide is more contentious still, and, when the terrain is social and political matters, becomes even harder to answer. Whilst there is no claim here to methodological superiority, the approach taken, the subjects covered, the conception of the terrain and the nature of the presentation all betoken a commitment to some of the properties most associated with an analytical approach. This is not only a reflection of the author's predilections but also of the dominant paradigm of political philosophy as practised in philosophy departments in the Anglo-American world. In this respect, the line taken in the second territorial dispute reflects something of the line taken in the first. It rests on the view that what analytical philosophers in political philosophy since Rawls have been doing is not thoroughly wrong-headed. It is not dreadfully vitiated by its foundationalism, made worthless by its failure to be self-reflective, and its pursuit of a paradoxically oppressive and exclusive road, in its insistence on rigour and transparency, and its failure to be playful and allusive.

So, insofar as terms, authors and theories are central to this enterprise – a largely normative enterprise, concerned with relations between individuals, groups and the state – they are central to the book. Insofar as they are more marginal to this enterprise, they will be less substantial in the book. Pareto will get a mention, but not as substantial an entry as Rousseau. The book reflects the state of play in the discipline. It centres on the Anglo-American tradition: so there are substantial entries not only on Rawls but also on reflective equilibrium, and on perfectionism. While centring on the Anglo-American tradition there will be substantial entries on, for example, Habermas, on deliberative democracy. There is substantial cross-referencing through the book, which will enable the reader to trace their way through a debate, fixing the major points of reference. Readers will be able to move through the book without discontinuities between the entries for thinkers, issues and positions. As well as terms, theories and theorists, there will be entries for any quirks of the discipline – so Wilt Chamberlain is the sole basketball player to get an entry.

Acknowledgements

I would like to thank the series editor Oliver Leaman, Carol Macdonald at EUP, and colleagues and students at the Open University especially those who tried out this material in draft form. I'm also grateful to Paul Harkin, Seth Crook and Derek Matravers who read the manuscript and made extensive helpful comments, and, especially, to Gillian Ure and Imogen Pike, who both made the experience of writing the book more pleasurable than it might otherwise have been: it is dedicated to them both.

Using this book

This book is designed to be a comprehensive, authoritative guide to one of the most important and widely taught branches of philosophy. It is both topical and historical, including entries on Hobbes, as well as on contract theory. It is primarily intended for students at undergraduate level where it is hoped that it will be useful both for beginners and for more advanced students. It aims to be a standard reference work which students will want to own alongside their course texts. *Political Philosophy from A–Z* is designed to work equally effectively with historical courses of the 'Plato to Nato' variety and with non-historical or themed courses, and courses in contemporary political philosophy.

Political Philosophy from A–Z should enable students to understand this terrain, because it links, contrasts and demarcates positions, thinkers and theories. So it will be clear how the *libertarianism* of *Anarchy State and Utopia* rests on an assumption of *self-ownership*, how the ensuing *entitlement theory* of *distributive justice* compares with an account of the *difference principle*, and how this principle is derived from *the original position*.

This level of interconnection means that readers will be able to pick up on a network of different terms and argument, and allow each entry to reach further than its 300-word limit might otherwise allow. So, the entry on Hobbes is comparatively brief, but the cross-referencing allows much wider exploration of his position through reference to natural right, natural law, state of nature and so on.

Political philosophy is sometimes tricky for undergraduates, since they bring a sense of the everyday political terrain from current affairs, but this matches badly to the terrain of the discipline. Rather than Democrats and Republicans, Labour and Conservative, students encounter communitarians and liberal-egalitarians, deliberative democrats and Lockeans. Readers will meet them all in this book.

Political Philosophy A–Z

A

abortion: The practice of deliberately ending a pregnancy is perhaps the most contentious issue in contemporary public culture, certainly in the US. Politically, the debate has become polarised between those who support 'a woman's right to choose', sometimes resting this on an account of bodily ownership, and those who assert the moral status of the foetus or embryo as a person, potential person, or human, and, therefore, inviolable. The former attitude is most common amongst feminists, the latter is widely held amongst the especially religious.

Other positions are possible. Some consequentialists bypass talk of the intrinsic status of the foetus or embryo, and discuss abortion as a matter of public policy, examining the costs and benefits of changing the law. Others view the question in terms of the constitutional processes by which abortion law might be changed. Still others, within moral philosophy, swerve away from general and abstract principles towards case-by-case discussion of whether a decision to abort can be the act of a virtuous agent.

As far as more general political philosophy goes, debates over abortion exemplify the pluralism of comprehensive views of the good that philosophers from **Berlin** to **Rawls** take as a starting point. Given that there are deeply held, considered and reasonable views that exclude each other, how ought our political institutions to be framed? One answer is that this can be done only on the basis of minimal rather than large agreement, and on the basis of a thin or political liberalism, that does not itself rest on any comprehensive moral or metaphysical view. Those who hold to a comprehensive moral view which is expressed in uncompromising views on abortion are unlikely to accept this account of the ways in which principles of political justice ought to be generated. They are likely to think that the liberal virtue of **toleration** ought not to be applied to those who seek to suppress women/murder children.

Further reading: Hursthouse 1987; Hursthouse 1991; Thomson 1971; Tooley 1972

absolutism: A system of rule in which there are no legal or authoritative limits on the reach of the ruler. The ruler may be an individual or the holder of an office – as is the case in an absolute monarchy. An absolute power will be practically limited, but not limited by rival institutions or agencies which claim political authority. Again, an absolute authority may choose not to intervene in wide areas of social life, but faces no legal obstacles if it does so choose to intervene (and in this way, a totalitarian government – which does intervene in all aspects of social life – can be seen as a subset of absolutist rule).

Key advocates of absolutism include Jean Bodin and Thomas **Hobbes,** as well as those such as Filmer who believed that monarchs ruled by **divine right**. The arguments for absolutism varied accordingly. For divine right theorists, God's agent on earth ought not to be hampered by merely man-made laws; for Hobbes, division and limitation of state power was too conducive to a strife that would unravel back to the state of nature to be countenanced.

Monarchical absolutism has been on the wane for centuries, but arguments over the nature and justification of limits on popular sovereignty are still live. Ought popular sovereignty to override the public/private divide, and what limits ought there to be on how a state can act in respect of minorities? What role is there for judicial review of government decisions? In each of these cases, an argument arises for restrictions on the power of the state. In each case, there can be an absolutist response: by what right is the will of the people restricted?

See **divine right; Hobbes, Thomas; tyranny of the majority**

Further reading: Skinner 1978

accidental distinction see **essential/accidental distinction**

accusatory system of justice: A system of natural jurisprudence in which accusations were made by private individuals rather than state prosecutors. The accuser would swear an oath to the truth of his charge, and seek support form other private individuals. The court of appeal was an ad hoc affair with no permanent or paid officials. The accusatory system of justice was banned by papal decree in 1215, but serves as a model for **John Locke** of the emergence of institutions of justice from the state of nature.

See **Locke, John; state of nature**

Further reading: Tully 1993

act-utilitarianism: Act-utilitarianism, which is distinguished from rule-utilitarianism, is a form of consequentialist moral view which asserts that agents are morally obliged to act in a way that secures the best consequences, expressed in terms of the greatest happiness or the greatest utility. In contrast to rule-utilitarians, act-utilitarians engage in moral evaluation on a case-by-case basis. A rule-utilitarian might endorse a general rule such as 'always tell the truth' because the rule was conducive – or at least more conducive than any other rule such as 'tell lies when you like' – to securing the best consequences. An act-utilitarian, in contrast, might easily suggest cases in which telling the truth would not be conducive to the best consequences. Under these circumstances, the act-utilitarian would prescribe breaking the rule to secure the best consequences, and the rule-utilitarian, prescribing obedience to the rule, would have to accept sub-optimal consequences. On this account, it looks as if, properly applied, act-utilitarianism rather than rule-utilitarianism is conducive to optimal consequences. But rule-utilitarians will be concerned with the qualification of proper application. On their argument, we ought to act according to rules that have the best consequence if internalised by the overwhelming majority.

See **consequentialism**

Further reading: Hooker 2000; Smart and Williams 1973; Scheffler 1988

adaptive preferences: If an individual's preferences are consistently out of line with the situation in which that individual finds themselves, then they will experience frustration and discontent. In order to avoid frustration and discontent, it is possible for them to adapt their preferences, either consciously or not, so that they are more in line with the individual's situation. Adaptive preferences of this sort seem to be a real phenomenon with supporting empirical evidence. However, they pose difficulties for any system of resource allocation in which preferences play a leading role: if preferences are adapted in order to conform to the situation people find themselves in, then they cannot be taken to indicate how individuals would structure their choices between different dominating situations. It is this criticism of adaptive preferences that has led some to look at more objective accounts of well-being, such as those taken in the **capabilities approach**.

See **capabilities approach**

Reading Elster 1983

affirmative action: Policy of amending **difference-blind liberalism** in order to secure advantages for previously disadvantaged groups. In particular, affirmative action (which is sometimes called positive discrimination) has involved changes in regulations to secure places in sought-after public institutions such as universities, the professions, and within political parties and public institutions for women and ethnically underrepresented groups. These may take the form of quotas, differential entry requirements, targeted recruitment and reserved spaces.

Affirmative action is contentious because it seems to go against impartial principles of justice. The underlying complaint that provides the supposed justification for affirmative action is that places in universities and public life ought to be distributed according to merit and not according to morally irrelevant criteria such as ethnicity. The fact that they have been distributed according to such morally irrelevant criteria is shown, *prima facie*, by the overwhelming preponderance of members of the majority ethnic group in these positions. Affirmative action seeks to remedy this apparent violation of the merit principle. However, according to some critics, it does so by infringing the merit principle itself, because it introduces ethnicity into selection procedures.

To resolve this tension, partisans try either to undermine affirmative action by downplaying the underlying problem and asserting the merit principle or, on the other side, justifying affirmative action by foregrounding the underlying problem, emphasising its injustice, and qualifying or amending the merit principle.

See **discrimination; justice**

Further reading: Boxill 1978; Edmonds 2006

alienation: According to Marx and later Marxists, alienation is a key feature of capitalist societies and it captures a sense in which what should be natural and familiar becomes foreign or alien to an individual. In the *Economic and Philosophical Manuscripts* of 1844, Marx describes four sorts of alienation. For the individual producer, Marx says, is alienated first from his product, second from the process or activity of production, third from his fellow man and fourth from his species being. In each case, something familiar becomes strange – the work of individual producers returns to dominate them and they become the 'plaything of alien forces'. This encourages feelings of competition and animosity towards fellow human beings with whom we ought to live familiarly, in harmony and cooperation.

Alienation has its roots in the two Hegelian notions of estrangement and externalisation. It is related to other sociological concepts – such as Durkheim's notion of anomie.

Controversy surrounds the extent to which alienation is a subjective or objective phenomenon. If it is subjective, then perhaps the resolution of alienation is not the overthrow of capitalist social relations but a process of cheering people up. If it is an objective phenomenon, then an error theory is needed to explain why some people lead meaningless lives but are still happy.

Alienation rests on an account of human nature, because it rests on assumptions about what is, or should be, familiar or natural to us, and what is unfamiliar, unnatural and alien. In doing so, it rests on some of the more opaque claims about what it is to be human. However, the critique of alienation is one of the parts of Marx's thought that has survived the experiments of the twentieth century to remain a potent criticism of capitalism.

See **commodity fetishism; historical materialism; Marxism**

Further reading: Elster 1985; Ollman 1971

altruism: Actions directed at, or motivated by, concern for the wellbeing of others, regardless of gains to the agent, are altruistic actions, and the opposite of egoistic actions. Altruism raises a number of problems.

First, are there, as a matter of fact, any genuinely altruistic actions? Psychological egoism is the view that denies the existence of genuinely altruistic actions. Those who hold this view aim to unmask seemingly altruistic acts as somehow answering to the needs and desires of the agent. Even self-sacrificial acts are to be explained by the resolution of a tension within the agent herself – who 'could not live with herself' for example, if she did not give up her life for her child.

Second, some sociobiologists have developed a notion of bio-altruism, in an endeavour to explain (for example) the warning cries of Vervet monkeys – actions which increase the risk to the individual monkey, but reduce the risk to the group. Kin selection – the tendency to favour altruistic actions towards one's own relatives also seems to fill an important explanatory gap. Without an account of bio-altruism, these constituted a problem for Darwinism.

Third, ought we to act altruistically? The answer seems obviously to be in the affirmative: most moral codes rest on concern for others, and condemn selfishness. But the view is controversial. It might be said that altruistic acts are praiseworthy (or supererogatory) but not obligatory, or that helping others can generate a culture of dependency, or that altruistic actions are in some other way self-defeating.

Hobbes is one of the strongest critics of altruism. For Hobbes, 'of the voluntary acts of every man, the object is some good to himself'. For David Gauthier, justice rests on a system of rules that depend on prudence.

Others, though, find the stark contrast between egoism and altruism to be an oversimplification. It seems obvious that my good can be, in some way, constituted by the good of others, that my life goes well when other lives go well. Therefore, when I aim at other lives going well, is that an altruistic or an egoistic view? In this way the dispute at the level of moral prescription rests on a difference at the level of social theory – just how much are we bound up, constituted by, and involved in the lives of others?

See **Hobbes, Thomas; prudence**

Further reading: Gauthier 1986; Seglow 2004

analytical Marxism: Analytical Marxism is a school of thought particularly associated with Professor Gerry Cohen of Oxford. His work *Karl Marx's Theory of History: A Defence* (1978) applied the standards of analytical philosophy to Marx's 1859 *Preface to a Critique of Political Economy*, and defended it as a form of functional explanation. The debate over the coherence of functional explanation was joined by, among others, John Elster and John Roemer who were working independently on the analytical foundations of Marxism: Roemer had a particular interest in formulating an account of exploitation that did not require any of the dubious metaphysical claims associated with the Labour

Theory of Value. Together with others, they formed an entirely new school in the Academy, known as Analytical Marxism, 'no-bullshit' Marxism, or, more specifically, as the September Group – which included Sam Bowles, Bob Brenner, Hillel Steiner, Philippe Van Parijs and Erik Wright. This group played an important role in altering the intellectual climate of political philosophy in Britain. Marxist thought had been influential in universities, but not in philosophy departments. The elusive nature of continental theorising and the aspirations of Marxism to 'scientific' status voiced by people like Althusser failed to penetrate far into analytical philosophy departments: the emergence of the journal *Radical Philosophy* had been one response to this hostility. The analytical Marxists changed this. Amongst other activities, G. A. Cohen, J. Elster and J. Roemer edited the influential series Studies in Marxism and Social Theory, published by CUP: its driving aspiration was that 'with the tools of non-Marxist social science and philosophy . . . Marxist thought will thereby be freed from the increasingly discredited methods and presuppositions which are still widely regarded as essential to it and that what is true and important in Marxism will be more firmly established' (Series Statement). However, Cohen's engagement with Marxism became increasingly critical. In particular, he became increasingly concerned about the impact of environmental constraints on the feasibility of a socialism based on abundance, and, second, about the 'obstetric metaphor' – that the new society was to be found in the womb of the old.

See **Cohen, Gerald A.; historical materialism**
Further Reading: Cohen 1978; Elster 1985

anarchism: It is sensible to divide anarchism into two phenomena – a political movement and a philosophical position.

The political movement, associated with Kropotkin and Bakunin and most powerful towards the end of the nineteenth century, is one of extreme hostility to the state. Hostile to the left notion of reforming the state or to the notion of a workers' state – political anarchism denies the state any legitimacy at all – anarchists prefer the idea of self-organised communities, attainable only after the (violent) overthrow of an oppressive state machine.

Philosophical anarchism is a position taken in debates about **political obligation** which asserts that there are no good reasons for obeying laws made by the state, as such. There may be independent moral grounds for those laws – they may be good laws that are morally binding because of their content. This view distinguishes between the thought that you ought not to kill people because it is wrong to do so and the thought that you ought not to kill people because it is against the law.

Philosophical anarchists, especially following Robert Paul Wolff, place a great deal of emphasis on autonomy and argue that granting any sort of right of obedience to the state involves an infringement of autonomy, and this is especially true in the case of a state based on representative rather than direct democracy.

Contemporary anarchism is influenced by and influences the ecological movement and feminism. In both cases, opposition to hierarchies is the common thread, whether those be hierarchies between men and women, hierarchies between human beings and nature or the hierarchies that are characteristic of the state.

Critics of anarchism tend to suggest that it rests on a false or utopian conception of human nature, or that it is light-minded about the complexities of social provision in a modern state, or that it grossly underestimates the importance that large numbers of people place on the welfare provisions of such states.

See **voluntarism**
Further reading: Wolff 1970

anthropocentrism: A theory of moral consideration that is centred on human beings. Unless anthropocentrists can identify a morally relevant property possessed by all humans and no other beings, then anthropocentrism is open to the charge that it is arbitrary and speciesist.

See **speciesism; zoocentrism**

aristocracy: Literally, rule by the best. In **Aristotle**'s politics, the contrast is drawn between oligarchy and aristocracy: both involve rule by the few, but oligarchy consists of rule by those few qualified by holdings of money, whereas aristocracy consists of those qualified by virtue.

Aristocracy is the middle of the three basic types of rule outlined by the Ancient Greeks – monarchy (rule by one) and democracy (rule by the people) are the other two. For Aristotle, in the *Politics*, aristocracy displayed some advantages but was inclined to collapse into oligarchy – rule by the wealthy few, in their own interests. However, the term has come to mean a form of rule in which those of a longstanding ruling class, distinguished by birth, property and an elite education, wield power. Its justification generally rests on some conception of natural or God-given order: for example, in the words of the English hymn:

> The rich man in his castle,
>   The poor man at his gate,
> God made them high or lowly,
>   And ordered their estate.

In *Reflections on the Revolution in France*, **Edmund Burke** endorses aristocratic rule as an outcome of respect for stable hierarchy, secured over many years. Support for aristocracy tends to fit well with conservative, organic and functional theories of society.

See **Aristotle; Burke, Edmund**

Aristotle (384–322 BCE) was a Greek philosopher and student of Plato. For Aristotle, man is a political animal – his distinctive form of functioning is as part of a state (although Aristotle had in mind a polis – a Greek city state) and he is at home and fully human in a political society. Politics is not something imposed on individuals from above – it is part of the natural state of affairs. Aristotle's defence of natural hierarchies led him to defend slavery, and the division of labour as natural and just. And the polis was always premised on the restriction of citizenship to free, native men.

Aristotle is a critic both of extreme democracy and of the tyranny – his ideal form of rule was an aristocracy, but this was an unstable form of rule. As a result, Aristotle prefers a mixed government in which citizens take turns in ruling and being ruled, with no dominant class of citizens.

Aristotle's most enduring contribution is probably his organic conception of the state. The isolated individual is not properly speaking human, since interdependence is a feature of the essentially human condition. Custom rather than fiat is a good basis for law, and political stability is one of the highest values, since only stability can provide the conditions for citizens to fulfil themselves as virtuous, contemplative beings who are fulfilled in political participation in a just state.

His key works are the *Politics*, and the *Nicomachean Ethics* and *Eudemian Ethics*. Contemporary Aristotelianism has seen something of a revival, both in terms of the resurgence of **virtue ethics**, but also in terms of some interesting neo-Aristotelian resonances in the capacities approach to economic inequality and in the communitarian insistence on the artificiality of the (supposedly) liberal model of human beings as atomised and abstracted individuals.

See **virtue ethics**

Further reading: Miller, Fred D. 1995; Mulgan 1977

assurance game: A model in game theory which expresses the idea of a virtuous circle. An assurance game generally involves two players, and shows the result of the existence of trust between them, based on the assurance received from past successful collaboration. Thus the players are able to secure a higher long-term pay off than if they competed, because of the existence of a history of trust. Assurance games contrast with **prisoner's dilemmas,** which can be expected to collapse into self-interested behaviour in which each player misses out on the gains of cooperation for fear that the other player will defect from cooperation first. Thus the short term trumps the long term and the gains of defection beat the gains of cooperation. Trust, assurance and reassurance alter this dynamic. The question is: how are they to be generated? The Hobbesian answer is that a powerful sovereign will enforce contracts, ensuring transition from the prisoner's dilemma of the state of nature into the assurance game of the commonwealth.

See **game theory; prisoner's dilemma; zero-sum game**

Further reading: Hampton 1986

atomism: In political philosophy, atomism is a term that works by analogy with the physical world. It chimes with the atomic account of the physical world first found from Democritus through Newton to the present day. When applied to the social and political world, atomism is a view that regards individuals as self-contained and self-sufficient units which constitute the building blocks of all larger social units. For atomists, the basic unit is the isolated individual.

Atomism, though, is usually a charge against social and political thinkers rather than a self-description. It is comparatively difficult to find a thinker who explicitly subscribes to this view, though **Hayek** and **Nozick** are prime candidates. The charge is most commonly made by Hegelians, Marxists and Communitarians, who object to a denial of the ways in which individuals are constituted by the social relations and contexts in which they find themselves. The key essay here is Charles Taylor's 'Atomism' (1985) in which he attacked what he characterised as the atomism underlying Nozick's work and counterposed the Aristotelian idea that 'Man is a social animal, indeed a political animal, because he is not self-sufficient alone, and in an important sense is not self-sufficient outside a polis' (Taylor 1985: 190).

Some different forms of the charge need to be distinguished. Atomism might be taken to refer to a methodological approach, where all explanation is supposed to take place by reference to individuals and their actions. Explanation in terms of classes or institutions needs, on this account, to be reduced to explanations couched solely in terms of individuals. This **methodological individualism** can usefully be contrasted with ethical individualism which focuses either on the claim that the ultimate ethical agent is the individual or on the claim that the individual ought to aim to promote his or her own interests rather than pursue the common good – a form of ethical egoism.

See **altruism; functionalism; methodological individualism**

Further reading: Taylor 1985

authority/authoritarianism: If a person or institution is authoritative, this means two things. First, they are the origin of certain judgements, claims, orders and so on – they are the author of these judgements in the same way that Tolstoy is the author of *War and Peace*. Second, the fact that they are the author of these judgements gives some reason for taking those judgements seriously – it gives them some weight. In authoritarianism's most clear form, an agent or group is authoritative if it has the right to do something, where the something includes requiring some action from others. In the social and political sphere, authority is asserted and questioned at the core of all political and social relations. The need for a theory of what makes an agent authoritative is clear.

Weber distinguished three types of authority: rational-legal, traditional and 'charismatic', and much political philosophy is concerned with the explication and justification of these types and the conflict between them. In particular, the development of Western democracies involves a shift from traditional to rational-legal authority, a shift which was the root of widespread disagreement and conflict. Plato's account of authority ends with the advocacy of philosopher-kings, and the condemnation of democracy: rule should be in the hands of those who are experts, not those who are popular. Divine right theorists, such as Filmer, explained authority in terms of a direct bequest of God's authority to temporal monarchs, whose line was established through inheritance. This was thought to be an expression of the natural order of things. Democratic theorists rest their account of authority on a voluntaristic basis. Since **Hobbes** and **Locke**, they tend to regard the individual human as the source of authority – perhaps devolved from God. They then explain political authority in the hands of the state (or monarch) in terms of some sort of contract which constitutes the authority and gives it its special status. **Philosophical anarchism** is critical of all claims to political authority on the basis that they necessarily undermine the fundamental autonomy of the individual.

In contrast, a political theory is authoritarian if it prescribes government based on established authority rather than the consent of the governed. Hobbes's account is authoritarian, since he prescribes obedience to existing authority, without inquiring into the legitimacy of its origins.

See **anarchism; autonomy; rights**

Further reading: Raz (ed.) 1990

autonomy: Self-rule – from the Greek *nomos*, meaning law or rule, and *auto*, meaning self. Just as an automatic car changes gear by itself, so an autonomous person rules himself. Autonomy is thought by many to be of basic value, since to treat someone as autonomous involves respecting them as a rational being with the right to make up their own mind as to how to live. Autonomy is contrasted with heteronomy – being ruled by someone or something else, and for philosophical anarchists this contrast lies at the root of the problem of political obligation. If we are obliged to follow rules made by others, then we can hardly be said to be autonomous beings. Thus autonomy and respect for others as autonomous beings conflicts directly with political authority. Others would not go so far.

Kant is perhaps the chief theorist of autonomy, though liberals in general raise autonomy as a key value. Autonomy seems to demand and ground rights, though some liberals, such as **Mill**, regard autonomy as only a guideline since it is generally conducive to the greatest good of the greatest number: we flourish if we are in conditions of autonomy. Again, conditions of autonomy feature in a kind of ideal theory, as a counterfactual claim about coercion claims. For example, we can ask whether a choice made by an individual is the same as one that would have been made under conditions of perfect autonomy. Autonomy thus comes into conflict with notions such as **false consciousness** and **adaptive preferences** – psychological claims about acting in conditions of freedom. It also seems to rest on prior assumptions about the debate on free will: whether libertarian ones, or compatibilist ones. Whatever its roots, the idea of autonomy is key for liberal thought. Sometimes it is so foundational that liberals are accused of raising autonomy as a meta-value, privileging it above other values (like community). This accusation looks stronger against perfectionist liberals than it does against anti-perfectionist ones.

See **deontology; justice; Kant**
Further reading: Dworkin 1988

B

Bentham, Jeremy (1748–1832) was a British Philosopher, legal theorist and economist. His most important work is the *Introduction to the Principles of Morals and Legislation* (1789). Bentham was the founder of utilitarianism according to which the aim of all legislation and social reform – in which he played an active part – ought to be the greatest happiness of the greatest number. Happiness was to be thought of as the presence of pleasure and the absence of pain, and this was to be ascertained in a quantitative manner through the 'felicific' or hedonic calculus. Bentham proposed that the calculus take account of factors such as intensity and duration, and the probability that an action or event would cause additional future pain or pleasure. The role played by laws was derived from this account: since the objective of governments was to secure the greatest happiness, laws ought to be conducive to that end. Those who break laws should be punished in order to deter them, and others, setting them back to activity conducive to the greatest happiness. Bentham conceives of the outcome of policy in a straightforwardly psychologically hedonistic way.

Bentham is also notable as a legal positivist, and as a critic of natural rights – which he famously denounced as 'nonsense on stilts'. Rights were not natural phenomena but the constructions of law: 'from real law come real rights, from imaginary laws come imaginary ones' (Bentham 1843; Harrison (ed.) 1998).

Bentham sets himself against natural rights theories, but also against that other opposition to absolutism – social contract theory. Real contracts, Bentham accepts, create real rights and obligations, but real contracts are a product of actual government and political and legal institutions. Therefore, they cannot be prior to, and a justification of, those institutions. Rather, the overall justification of political society is couched in terms of its benefits: we ought to calculate whether the 'probable mischiefs of obedience are less than the probable mischiefs of resistance' (Bentham 1843; Bentham 1988).

Embalmed, Bentham's body is on display in University College, London.

See **consequentialism; utilitarianism**

Further reading: Bentham 1988; Rosen 1983

Berlin, Isaiah (1909–97): Originally from a Latvian Jewish family, Isaiah Berlin is one of the most celebrated contributors to political thought of the twentieth century. Berlin developed no system of his own, and his contribution lies more in the history of political thought than in political philosophy as an analytical discipline. Berlin is famed for insisting on the plural nature of moral values – in opposition to monism, the idea that there is one supreme value, one best way of living, and one set of rules to cover them. This value of **pluralism** sponsors opposition to any overarching or perfectionist account of human nature. Moreover, Berlin opposes attempts to realise or actualise such monist accounts by reforming social institutions so that they fit with the monist account. Instead, Berlin argued, politics ought to be a practice that fits with the 'crooked timber of humanity' – in **Kant**'s phrase, and he finds moral pluralism as far back as **Machiavelli**. He saw in **Rousseau** and **Marx** harbingers of the totalitarianism of the twentieth century, because of their worrying emphasis on 'positive freedom'. Berlin also wrote on the German romantic tradition of Vico and Herder, and was most famed in his life time for his small book on Marx.

See **perfectionism; pluralism; positive liberty**
Further reading: Ignatieff 1998

brute luck/option luck: A pair of terms coined by Ronald Dworkin to model a sophisticated version of **luck egalitarianism**. Brute luck concerns the effects of simple chance, unmediated by individual choice, on a person's life, such as being struck by lightning. Option luck refers to the chance outcomes of autonomous choices made by an individual, such as suffering high losses at the roulette table, having made a free and deliberate choice to gamble. According to luck-egalitarians, justice requires compensation for the effects of brute luck but not for the effects of option luck.

The problem with the distinction is that it seems parasitic on views about free will and determinism that are highly contested. Gambling addicts may wish to claim that they are victims of brute luck: in contrast, someone who chooses to take a walk in a thunderstorm may be acting recklessly. If, in the end, the determinists are right, then all luck is brute luck, and luck-egalitarians will favour absolute equality. Otherwise some slippery metaphysical concepts will play a large part in determining a just distribution of resources.

See **luck egalitarianism**

Further reading: Dworkin 1981a; Dworkin 1981b

Burke, Edmund (1729–97): Burke was an Irish-born theorist of conservatism and opponent of the French Revolution, MP, and a leading parliamentary orator. In his major work, *Reflections on the Revolution in France*, Burke outlines an organic conception of the state, advocacy of slow and piecemeal reform (if it takes place at all), and protests at the violent excesses of the revolutionaries. Burke is regarded as the founder of modern conservative thought.

See **conservatism**

Further reading: Burke 1985; Macpherson 1980

C

capabilities approach: This is an approach to distributive justice which places human capabilities, rather than bundles of goods, at the centre of concern. The key task for just distributive arrangements is to allow those capabilities to be made actual. This means, for example, that additional resources ought to be distributed to those with disabilities, since they will require greater resources in order to actualise their capabilities. The principle is generalisable – it directs attention to the fact that individuals may be differently able to use resources in order to bring themselves up to a common level of welfare, and it suggests that this consideration ought to weigh in calculations of distributive justice.

Actualisation of capabilities is the measure by which distributive arrangements are to be judged. The approach is particularly associated with Martha Nussbaum and Amartya Sen, and is of some significance for policy formation on a global scale – Sen's approach has a role in the UN through the United Nations Development Programme on Capability Indicators. Often, advocates of the capabilities approach find themselves giving a list of human capabilities and arguing about which capabilities on the list are essential to human flourishing and which are not. The approach has its roots in **Aristotle**'s commitment to human flourishing.

Some have argued that the capabilities approach relies too heavily on arbitrary assertions about human nature and the good life, and so imposes an ethnocentric account of human flourishing on diverse individuals and groups. Can hermits or nomads flourish? If they can, then almost all material goods, permanent shelter and social interaction are not essential to the actualisation of central capacities. If they can't flourish, this seems ethno-centric. One response to this criticism is to hollow out the conception of human nature on which the capabilities approach rests. But this risks reducing the theory to practical emptiness. Other, more applied, criticisms concern the degree to which capabilities are measurable, and the suggestion that, for policy purposes, the capabilities approach collapses into more conventional forms of welfare provision and policy.

Further reading: Nussbam and Sen 1993; Sen 1995

capitalism: A system of rules and distributive arrangements based on private ownership and a market economy. Capitalism particularly involves private ownership of the means of production and, generally, finds those means of production held in the hands of a minority of the population. Consequently capitalist social relations are relations of monetary exchange – of money for goods and of labour for money. Capitalism is thought by its proponents to be uniquely suited to human freedom, and to non-hierarchical relations, but its opponents tend to point to the very widespread resource and income inequality to which it leads, and the exploitation and alienation that they assert it involves.

Both empirically, and in theory, there are reasons for associating mature capitalism with relatively mature, relatively fluid democratic societies, and also for associating it with rapid technological development generated through the competition that arises from the free consumer market. However, this is associated with various ills – consumerism (and the particular Marxist variant of this – commodity fetishism).

Distinctively, capitalism organises production for profit, rather than for the direct satisfaction of human need. In Marx's classical formulation, capitalism works by extracting surplus value from labour: human labour is distinctive in that it is the sole generator of value. But the worker's labour power is sold to the capitalist, and value is extracted from him by the capitalist, in return for the means of subsistence. Because of the paucity of alternatives available to the labourer, this looks like exploitation.

However, advocates of capitalism argue that, contrary to expectations, it does better at serving human needs, in a roundabout way, than any other possible competing arrangement, because of side effects such as increased productivity, increased innovation, and the trickling down of benefits.

See **Hayek, Friedrich August von; Marx, Karl; Nozick, Robert; property**

Further reading: Elster and Moene 1989; Nozick 1974

care ethics: An interest in an ethics specifically related to care emerges from the debate between Kohlberg and Gilligan (*In a Different Voice*, 1982) and from independent developments in moral theory – in particular, a return to discussion of **virtue ethics**, following Anscombe's paper 'Modern Moral Philosophy' (1958). Gilligan's analysis of moral development emerges from empirical results about gender differences in thinking about justice. Small boys thought in universal terms, girls in particular ones, especially thinking about specific relations to named individuals, and responsibility and ties of affection with those individuals. Gilligan later withdrew the claim that the distinction between an ethic of care and an ethic of justice was empirically founded.

Care ethics concentrate on actual relationships between persons and are not necessarily universally applicable. They involve giving value to emotional and empathic identification with particular people, valuing friendship and companionship, individual care (of children, of the sick, of the elderly) associated with virtue ethics and the ethics of **Aristotle**. One way of understanding the point of an ethics of care is to reflect on the response to thanking someone for visiting you in hospital and receiving the reply – 'well, it's what morality and duty demanded'.

In one way, care ethics is anti-political, because it seeks to reorientate ethical thinking away from its public, general and enforceable terrain, concerned with a conception of the just society and how its laws should be, to everyday interactions between people.

Nevertheless, care ethics has been influential in political philosophy – critical of the focus on impersonal and impartial principles of justice, and influential on the critique of Rawlsian justice offered by **Iris Marion Young**, Elisabeth Anderson and others. Young argues against the notion of impartiality as such, pushing the attack on impartialism in the private sphere further into the realm of politics.

See **virtue ethics**

Further reading: Barry 1995; Gilligan 1982

categorical imperative: Term used to describe the key principle of **Kant**'s ethical theory, and the guiding principle of Kantian moral theory as it relates to political life. The categorical imperative is found in Kant's *Groundwork to the Metaphysic of Morals* (1785) and comes in three forms. First it takes the form of a general principle that one ought to *act only according to that maxim by which you can at the same time will that it should become a universal law.*

In its second formulation, the categorical imperative is to act *in such a way that you always treat humanity, whether in your own person or in the person of any other, never simply as a means, but always at the same time as an end.*

In its third formulation, the categorical imperative is to *act as though you were through your maxims a law-making member of a kingdom of ends.*

In terms of political philosophy, the Kantian categorical imperative has been widely cited and used. It falls most happily in line with opposition to utilitarian accounts of authority and public policy. In particular, the second formulation runs up against several ways in which a simple **utilitarianism** prescribes actions that threaten justice (for example, punishment of the innocent in circumstances where that would be the action most conducive to general well-being). The categorical imperative sits well, too, with the separateness of persons which is emphasised by liberal and libertarian thinkers – the second formulation expresses well some intuitions brought to the fore by consideration of the **eye lottery** case. For that reason, it can seem to be part of an argument against redistributive taxation. Similarly, the categorical imperative can put limits on state enforcement of our obligations to others, and so prescribe some general boundaries between the state and the citizen. For this reason, it has been central to some formulations of liberal thought. Most recently, Kant's imprecation has found rigorous development in the contractualist moral theory outline by Scanlon.

See **deontology; Kant, Immanuel**

Further reading: Flikschuh 2000; O'Neill 1990; Scanlon 2000

circumstances of justice: The circumstances of justice are the conditions that are jointly necessary and sufficient for justice to be required. If there are circumstances of justice then there are at least possible, and perhaps actual, worlds in which justice is not required. Equally, the circumstances of justice will prescribe the kinds of problems that justice is required to resolve. Political Philosophers from **Aristotle**, to **Hume, Kant, Marx** and **Rawls** have had something to say about the circumstances of justice. For Aristotle, justice was sometimes counterposed to friendship; amongst friends there is no need for justice. Hume's account in *An Enquiry Concerning the Principles of Morals*, Section III Part 1, is the *locus classicus* for contemporary discussions. In this account, Hume suggests that there are both objective and subjective conditions of justice. If there is absolute abundance of some good, such as air, then there is simply no need for principles of justice in order to determine its distribution. At the other end of the scale, and more controversially, if there is so little of some essential good that life is at stake, then justice becomes a luxury to be dispensed with.

But the conditions of justice are also subjective: scarcity denotes a gap between what is available and what is wanted, and wants can vary. A world in which commodities seem to bestow power and in which a competitive and zero-sum struggle for status is part of the fabric of society is one in which principles of justice will be required. So too, when there are dramatic inequalities of power.

Marx and others have argued that the circumstances of justice are historically specific – consequently that the rights of man are the rights of egoistic man. Whatever might be the case about economic abundance – and growing ecological concern suggests that optimism here might be misplaced – recent philosophers such as Rawls have highlighted competing conceptions of the good life as one of the irreducible background considerations which drive and require a theory of justice.

In another possible world, four things might be different. First, it is conceivable that there could be very great material abundance. Secondly, and alternatively, there could be very great self-restraint and altruism. This is an alternative to abundance in the following way: the need for restraint and altruism varies inversely with the level of abundance, but at the poles – absolute abundance or absolute self-restraint – there is no need for a corresponding level of self-restraint or abundance respectively. Thirdly, it is conceivable that there could be only one, generally agreed, conception of the good (or a few conceptions that were congruent in all their material consequences). Perhaps there could be only one conception of the good, because there could, in fact, only be one good, and in some way this good life for man has been discovered. Fourthly, it is conceivable that there could be knowledge of congruent preferences that is so near to perfect that conflict over the means of securing the good would come to an end. The exact relation between these four conditions is a little contentious – whether they are jointly necessary for justice, or only individually necessary. Nevertheless, it is clear that, in a world marked by these conditions, or one like it, there would be much less need for careful thinking about distributive justice.

See **distributive justice; justice**

Further reading: Lukes 1987

civic republicanism: Civic republicanism is a term for a variety of political thought with a long history. It refers to a democratic and participative tradition which draws on insights found in **Aristotle**, Cicero and **Machiavelli** through to **Rousseau, Wollstonecraft** and James Madison. In these writers, civic republicanism involves recognition of the necessary interdependence of human beings, and an account of freedom that is arguably richer than the liberal focus on the absence of external constraint. If our lives are necessarily interdependent, then, in the face of mutual vulnerability, we share a common fate. Political participation is the key to determining that common fate and, even more, to securing meaningful freedom.

Civic republicanism then focuses on common goods and political involvement in contrast to the liberal emphasis on individual interests and rights. In this respect it is akin to **communitarianism**, but there are differences. Whereas communitarians tend to rely on pre-existing community values, civic republicans pay more attention to the way in which values emerge through a deliberative process.

Civic republicanism predates liberalism but owes the resurgence in its significance to the eclipse of the conflict between liberalism and socialism. It works as a critique of **liberalism**, but is posed at the philosophical and political level, rather than being primarily concerned with economic inequalities and exploitation. Prominent advocates of civic republicanism and critics of liberalism on this sort of basis include Hannah Arendt and Charles Taylor.

The focus on political participation is in one way distinctive and in another way not. Emerging from the liberal-communitarian debate, some liberals acknowledge the importance of participation as an instrument to secure individual liberties as individuals pursue separate ends. But this contrasts with a view which foregrounds participation as a key independent value regardless of its effects – a view known as civic humanism.

See **positive liberty; Rousseau, Jean-Jacques**
Further reading: Honohan 2002

coercion: Someone is coerced if they are made to do something against their will. However, coercion must be distinguished from compulsion. A paradigm case of compulsion occurs when someone is physically manipulated into an action whilst resisting that action. For example, if someone is literally chained and restrained, and either manipulated into an act or subjected to an act, then they are compelled. Less clear-cut cases of coercion are involved when physical compulsion is absent, but the possible coercer alters the options available to an individual in order to ensure a certain outcome. Normally, this will be by means of a threat, designed to increase the costs of the least-favoured option. In this case, the degree to which coercion is involved depends on the alternatives on offer. A judgement is required of the coerced person, that it was not reasonable to expect her to resist the pressure applied to undertake the action sought by the coercer. At what point is it clear that the coerced person is offered 'no choice'?

The coercer alters the cost of the alternatives available to the coercee by ensuring that the sought alternative is much less costly than the alternative, which is expressed as a threat. Thus the coercer may offer a (real choice): your money or your life.

Further reading: Wertheimer 1987

Chamberlain, Wilt: Wilt Chamberlain was a basketball player. In the famous Wilt Chamberlain example, **Nozick** aims to show that free exchanges of resources will lead to instabilities in any pattern of resource distribution. Because the exchanges are uncoerced, there can be no complaint against them, and no injustice in a process that leads to inequality. By employing a modified version of **Locke**'s account of appropriation, he aims to establish that widespread inequalities of holdings between individuals cannot be justly broken down by redistributive tax policies. This is because taxation is a form of forced labour, and so infringes the rights of individuals. The upshot of Nozick's argument is that intuitions about equality are trumped by intuitions about self-ownership and the property rights that these intuitions entail.

Cohen, Gerald A.: Canadian philosopher and Chichele Professor of Political Theory at All Souls College, Oxford. Whilst teaching at University College, London, Cohen established his reputation with *Karl Marx's Theory of History: A Defence* (1978) which presented and defended an account of historical materialism in an analytical manner. With the book Cohen founded a school of **Analytical Marxism**, although he gradually moved away from his concern with **Marxism** towards normative political philosophy. First, in *Self-Ownership, Freedom and Equality* (1995), he criticised the assumption of self-ownership which underpinned Nozick's entitlement theory of justice. Then in *If You're an Egalitarian, How Come You're So Rich?* (2000), he criticised the limits on the egalitarianism found in Rawls's *Theory of Justice*. He argues for a form of **luck egalitarianism**, and for the need for an egalitarian ethos: it is not enough simply to ensure that institutions are just.

See **functionalism; historical materialism; luck egalitarianism; self-ownership**

Further reading: Cohen 1978; Cohen 1986; Cohen 2000

communitarianism: Communitarianism is an approach to political philosophy that places a great deal of emphasis on the importance and strength of communities, cultures and traditions in the formation of political identities. However, rather than being a well-defined position it is more a tendency of thought, characterised by the idea that **liberalism** overestimates the individual as the bearer of value at the expense of communal goods.

Philosophical communitarianism is specifically associated with criticism of the 'unencumbered self' which is supposed by some communitarians to be core to classical liberal thought. The 'unencumbered self' is the self without community ties or allegiances, ageless and genderless, and without a comprehensive conception of the good life. On some accounts, the unencumbered self is the building block of liberalism, the sort of individual best placed to select principles of justice. Against this picture, communitarians doubt the possibility – and coherence – of being unencumbered in this way, and so doubt the possibility of constructing a theory of justice that is prior to a theory of the good. The term is associated with the work of Charles Taylor, Michael Sandel, **Alasdair MacIntyre** and **Michael Walzer**. However, each of them has been less than enthusiastic about endorsing the label. Sandel's text Liberalism and the Limits of Justice is the key starting point for the communitarian critique of **Rawls,** whilst MacIntyre and Walzer direct their criticism at aspects of modern culture more generally.

Political communitarianism expresses the common complaint that contemporary social life lacks 'a sense of community' and the desire to recover it. It is best represented by Amitai Etzioni's *The Spirit of Community* (1993), and William Galston's work. Political communitarianism emphasises that rights need to be balanced by responsibilities, and opposes a culture of egoism and individualism and promotes the community, the family and opposition to social disintegration – for example, the promotion of community based action as a way to combat crime. Political communitarianism, though, is some distance from philosophical communitarianism.

See **liberalism; Marxism; Rawls, John**

Further reading: Etzioni 1993; Macintyre 1981; Sandel 1985; Swift and Mulhall 1992; Taylor 1989; Walzer 1983

community: Generally, community refers to any relatively stable social group, based on or differentiated by, more or less any characteristic. However, the word also has a more technical use in **John Locke**'s Second Treatise. For Locke, the community is what emerges from the **state of nature.** The community entrusts its interests to a government and it is the job of the government to serve the interests of the community. Communities are relatively stable, according to Locke, so that a change of government does not mean that the crisis of political power will unravel right the way back to an antagonistic state of nature.

consent: Consent is a key term in contemporary political philosophy because of the widespread concern with treating individuals as persons, a concern which has its roots in **Kant** and **Locke**. If I am to treat you with respect for your personhood, then, before I undertake any act which may affect you, I need to have your consent. This seems to apply in clear cases of ethical concern, from sexual behaviour (intercourse without consent is rape) to medical practices, where medical intervention without consent is contrary to many ethical codes, even if in the patient's best interests, to questions of political authority – where legitimacy seems to rely on some sort of consent given by the governed.

But this last example highlights some of the problems: if legitimate government is based on consent, then can I not withdraw my consent to the parking restrictions outside my house, in order to deprive them of their legitimacy? What if we all did that? Making individual consent a necessary condition for the legitimacy of the state seems to be too strong. But weakening the requirement in the direction of tacit consent or hypothetical consent seems to water down the attraction of the original problem-solving idea.

Again, is consent given in an informed way? Consent based on false or partial information seems not to carry with it the binding effects between the consenter and the outcome that she has consented to. But who is under the responsibility to secure the fully informed consent of the individual in question, and what are the limits to this responsibility? Sometimes it is said that consent is binding only if it is secured 'under conditions of autonomy'. But the implications of insisting on these ideal world constraints might be that there is very little genuine consent on offer in the real world.

See **authoritarianism; express consent; Locke; John; Plamenatz, John; tacit consent; voluntarism**

Further reading: Plamenatz 1968

consequentialism: Consequentialism is a term first used by Elisabeth Anscombe in 1958 to cover a range of theories according to which the moral value of an act or other moral entity is derived solely from its consequences. Clearly, consequentialists need to say what it is about the consequences that constitute moral worth. Are the consequences an increase in human happiness, or a maximisation of preference satisfaction, or experiences of beauty? Consequentialism itself leaves open the criterion of moral worth, and so covers a family of views, most notably **utilitarianism.**

However, it does rule other views out – such as the view that the moral worth of an act derives from its being in accordance with some rule such as the **categorical imperative,** or its being carried out from a sense of duty, or its being the sort of act characteristically carried out by a virtuous agent.

This gives rise to a difficulty for all consequentialist thought – that it seems to conflict with justice, if it is the case that an unjust act can have good consequences. Even if, in practice, this can be ruled out, still, the prohibition on unjust acts ought (anti-consequentialists argue) to arise from the fact that they are unjust, not because they happen to have bad consequences.

There is also controversy over whether consequentialism is supposed to act as a decision procedure or a criterion of rightness. If it is the former, then it looks impracticable in a world in which infinite, unforeseen consequences ripple out from an act. If it is the latter, then a criterion of rightness which one never knows one has met seems worse than useless.

Nonetheless, consequentialism is attractive if we require that moral and political action is rooted in and valued on the basis of the actual changes – the consequences – that actions bring into being, and this is a plausible thought.

See **deontology; Mill, John Stuart; utilitarianism; virtue ethics**

Further reading: Anscombe 1958; Scheffler 1988

conservatism: To call conservatism a political philosophy is rather to overstate the case. Rather, conservatism is a tradition in political thought, characterised by perhaps three key features.

The first is scepticism about reform: the currently existing state of things is thought by conservatives to contain historic wisdom, and proposals to reform the existing order are fraught with risk. This scepticism extends both to abstract reasoning about the principles governing human affairs – conservatives preferring the more solidly empirical approach – and scepticism towards any sort of radical or revolutionary change.

Second, conservatism often rests on an organic conception of society and the state, where each element functions for the good of the whole. This is both an explanatory notion and a normative one: it can require that what an individual ought to do is to discover his or her role, and then perfom it.

Thirdly, conservatism is deferential towards established authority without inquiring too deeply into the sources of that authority. It is, consequently, hostile to the social contract tradition of **Locke, Hobbes** and **Rousseau**.

Lastly, conservatism tends to favour what it sometimes sees as natural hierarchies. Contemporary conservatives such as Roger Scruton and John Kekes express many of these themes, but they also target the egalitarianism which is a strong strand in contemporary political philosophy

See **Aristotle; Burke; Edmund; Nozick, Robert**

Further reading: Kekes 1999; Scruton 1980

contextualism: A school of thought in the history of political philosophy particularly associated with Cambridge University according to which the social historical political and literary context of a text is essential to a proper understanding of its meaning. The term is perhaps most associated with Quentin Skinner who launched a ferocious attack on much work of interpretation of historical texts in 'The Limits of Historical Explanation (1966, in Tully [ed.] 1989). In this he showed that a variety of interpreters had included anachronistic and ahistorical claims in their work, arising from an ahistorical methodology. Influenced by Wittgenstein, Skinner argued that writing political works was an illocutionary act – and in order to understand the meaning of the act it was essential to understand the questions that an author was addressing, and the texts to which he was responding. Others influenced by the school include John Dunn, James Tully and Richard Tuck. A key moment in the development of the Cambridge or Contextual school came when Peter Laslett showed that **Locke's** two *Treatises on Civil Government* were written not after the revolution of 1688, as a *post hoc* rationalisation of the new regime, but in fact between 1679–83, as a revolutionary tract, in effect prescribing revolutionary acts against the state.

The contextual school contributes greatly to our understanding of the complex matrix of intentions, responses, questions and influences that inform a writer's intent in reading a work. But the suggestion that there is a single methodological key to understanding a text, and that there was nothing to be learned from a self-consciously ahistorical account based on rational reconstruction, is now out of favour. Philosophers now tend to argue for methodological pluralism in which the approach to determining the interpretation of a text depends critically on the questions which one asks of it.

Further reading: Tully (ed.) 1989.

contract theory: If political philosophy is a normative practice, then it will spend much of its time assessing what obligations and duties we have. Obligations may have many sources, but, roughly speaking, they might be natural or constructed. If they are constructed, this might be because persons make promises to each other. Promising generates obligations, and the idea of a contract is a generalisation and formalisation of the practice of promising. Thus contract theory is important because contracts are an archetypal way of establishing obligations, and obligations give us rules that can apply generally – hence, for those who find the idea of natural obligations inadequate or mysterious, contractualism can seem to be the root of all normative thinking in political philosophy.

control/income rights: Distinction introduced by John Christman into discussions of **distributive justice**. The right of private property is in fact an aggregation of several specific individual rights, so that one can distinguish fuller and weaker theories of private property depending on which particular nest of rights they ascribe to the property owner. Christman's distinction is between those rights required to control the use of a thing and rights over the income generated by that thing. If the distinction works, it shows how someone can own – in the sense of controlling – a thing, without that ownership leading to very wide inequalities of wealth since the property owner does not own the rights to profit from the use of the thing. In this way, the distinction between control and income rights underpins an attempt to bring together **self-ownership** rights (construed as control rights) with a concern for economic equality and redistributive taxation policies (since the income rights do not sit with the owner of the control rights). This allows a reconciliation of concerns about equality with concerns about autonomy and self-ownership, a reconciliation that is the aim of left-libertarians.

See **libertarianism; property**

Further reading: Christman 1994a; Christman 1994b

conventional rights see **natural rights/conventional rights**

cosmopolitanism/cosmopolitan justice: The view, most famously articulated by **Kant**, in *Perpetual Peace* (1795), that advocates a world state and world government that transcends and replaces nation states. The ideal has Stoic roots, expressed in the claim of Diogenes Laertius, 'I am a citizen of the world'. More abstractly, cosmopolitans favour supra-national law and cosmopolitan institutions of justice which implement universal standards of justice. Cosmopolitanism is clearly opposed to realist accounts of international relations and involves generalising arguments about justice from the level of the nation state to the level of the world as a whole. It thus tends to dissolve the distinction between distributive theories of justice organised on a national basis (such as that of **Rawls** in *A Theory of Justice* [1971]) and the whole perspective of international (rather than global) justice as such. For Thomas Pogge, cosmopolitanism has three components: *individualism* – human beings rather than family lines, tribes, ethnic, cultural, or religious communities, nations, or states are the proper objects of concern; *universality* – this concern is due to every living human being *equally; generality* – the concern is due *from* everyone in the same way.

Amongst contemporary cosmopolitan thinkers are Martha Nussbaum, Brian Barry and David Held. Nussbaum argues that cosmopolitanism does not displace particular attachments to kin, but augments them, whilst

Held speculates on world government and the possibilities of thoroughgoing institutional reform.

Further reading: Caney 2006; Nussbaum 1999

D

deliberative democracy: An account of democracy that foregrounds deliberation, discussion and dialogue directed towards agreement. Deliberative democracy is generally contrasted with pictures of democratic decision making in which citizens are polled on their preferences, with no need or obligation to take part in a deliberative process. The term originates from Joseph Bessette in 'Deliberative Democracy: The Majority Principle in Republican Government' (1980), and is also associated with proposals and arguments presented by Jon Elster, Amy Gutmann and Joshua Cohen, and it draws on Habermas's conception of ideal discourse. One model of deliberative democracy is the jury system in criminal trials. Some proponents of deliberative democracy make reference to the ways in which deliberation can improve the quality of the decisions made. This justifies deliberative processes as a better instrument for making decisions – decisions will be more effective, or better judged, or morally sound if they are made through deliberative processes. Others, drawing on historical traditions going back to **Aristotle** regard deliberation and participation as intrinsic goods.

Amongst deliberative instruments are citizens' juries, public meetings, focus groups and online communities with decision-making powers. Deliberative democrats characteristically tie the legitimacy of decisions to the deliberative process, arguing that, without the opportunity for participation in a deliberative process, decisions cannot be authoritative, even if they reflect the majority opinion. Recording the process, too, is central to the deliberative agenda. There is congruence between this view and the account of moral justification given by Tim Scanlon, in that deliberative democracy draws attention to the reasons given for a particular view, not simply the preferences of those who have a chance to vote. In particular, the reasons need to be publicly presented – and not capable of reasonable rejection by those who are the victims of the decision. In this way, deliberative democracy is designed to achieve the consensus that is essential to a decision being authoritative. The relation between deliberative democracy and voting procedures is an underdeveloped area, however.

See **civic republicanism; democracy**

Further reading: Pressette 1980; Cohen, Joshua 1997; Elster, Jon 1997

democracy: Democracy is a system of government in which the people (Greek 'demos') rule. Its origins lie in fifth-century Athens, the first democracy, where decisions were taken by a variety of democratic methods, including assemblies and the drawing of lots. A number of different models of democracy can be distinguished. Direct and indirect models are distinguishable according to whether there is an intermediary between the voter and the decision. Contemporary liberal democratic assemblies of elected representatives are forms of indirect democracy, one form of which is representative democracy. Telephone voting for game shows is a form of direct democracy, closely related to participatory democracy. Recent theorists have placed more emphasis on the processes of discussion and reflection involved in making democratic decisions, and constructed models of **deliberative democracy**.

Democracy is marked by an assumption of equality between the participants in the decision-making process, though also by the drawing of lines between those who participate and those who do not. Fifth-century Athenian democracy included men, but excluded women, slaves and foreigners, and contemporary democracies exclude children and sometimes prisoners, or bankrupts, or various other categories of would-be voters.

Democracy is thought to be closely related to legitimacy and the justification of political obedience, especially on the basis of voluntaristic assumptions about legitimacy. How can someone reasonably be expected to obey a government when she had no place in selecting it? Democratic governments provide a way of weakening the threat to autonomy that is involved in being governed at all.

Plato is the most famous philosophical opponent of democracy. In *The Republic*, he asks why those who lack knowledge of statecraft should be entrusted with the running of the state. He presents an analogy with sailing a ship. It would be dangerous and absurd to allow the whole crew to determine the course of a ship: it is rational to entrust this task to expert navigators and helmsmen: the same goes for states.

Simple majoritarian democracies face the criticism that they pay insufficient attention to the rights or interests of minorities: democracies involve the 'tyranny of the majority'. A persistent minority is not respected and this shows that the minority cannot be autonomous since it is ruled by a rule it didn't make itself.

The problem of minorities gives rise to a paradox of democracy: the supporter of democracy who also supports a minority viewpoint seems to be committed to saying that they support outcome A because it is the majority view, and they support outcome not-A because that is the minority view with which they agree.

See **deliberative democracy**

Further reading: Wollheim 1962

democratic centralism: Democratic centralism is the key organisational principle of Leninist politics. The term democratic centralism was most clearly explicated in *What Is to Be Done?* (1902) – and Lenin summarised the doctrine as '[f]reedom of discussion, unity of action'. For Leninists, democratic centralism prescribes the way in which a 'combat' party, engaged in a fierce political struggle, ought to operate, by maintaining internal freedoms, but presenting a united face to the world.

At the time of *What Is to Be Done?*, democratic centralism played a part in provoking the split with the Menshiviks, and was also opposed by Leon Trotsky, who argued for a more open organisation. In practice the idea of democratic centralism has been open to huge abuse, since the balance between the democratic element and the centralist element is not formally specified. The idea is that discussions are free up to the point of a vote, in which the majority decides the line taken by the entire party. But this means that questions cannot be reopened in the light of changing events, and it seems to assume that majorities are stable. What is more, democratic centralism does not make any space for recognition of a plurality of sincerely held conceptions of the good. All of this seems problematic in theory and practice. In fact, the Bolshevik Party moved away from democratic centralism towards straight centralism and absolute authority on the part of the leadership very early in its life, with many critics dating the abandonment of the principle to the Ban on Factions at the Xth Party congress of the Bolshevik Party in 1921.

See **deliberative democracy; democracy**
Further reading: Lenin [1902] 1988

deontology: Name given to a species of ethical theory that places duty at the core of moral value. Deontology is particularly associated with **Kant**, and with the idea that a set of moral prescriptions that is objectively true, generally in the form of a set of rules, can be proposed by rational and conceptual analysis, not empirical inquiry. In this way, and many others, deontological ethics is opposed to the two other great species of ethical theory – **consequentialism** and **virtue theory**, both of which give a role to the empirical. Deontological theories insist upon our duties to treat others as rational beings.

Deontological ethics focuses on how we ought to treat each other, given that we are rational and autonomous beings. One short answer is that we ought to treat people precisely as rational and autonomous beings, which we fail to do if we treat them solely as a means to an end that they cannot share. This, and other forms of the same basic idea, expressed in the **categorical imperative** form the basis of the deontological approach to politics. Such restrictions on how we ought to treat each other fit well with theories of human rights (though these can have a non-deontological grounding) and with the liberal idea of limited government, and the key role of consent in determining what is and is not politically justifiable. If I consent to your actions (and I am consenting under conditions of autonomy) then you are entitled to act. If I do not consent, then you are treating me instrumentally. Furthermore, Kantian ethics of this sort seems to underpin an emphasis on reasonable persuasion rather than coercion as a key value – it seems, then, a good fit with many democratic presumptions.

Critics of deontology point out that it is possible to found a liberal democratic polity on a quite different basis (though it might be doubted whether the foundations are so secure) and point to the austere and unforgiving prescriptions of some deontologists, including **Kant** himself. The abstraction of deontology can be contrasted unfavourably with the down-to-earth approach taken by utilitarians, and the way in which virtue theory captures our intuitions about special duties to particular people – our own parents or children, for example.

See **consequentialism; Kant, Immanuel; virtue ethics**
Further reading: O'Neill 1990

descriptive see **normative/descriptive**

desert: Desert is, perhaps surprisingly, a concept whose place and status in political philosophy is controversial. It seems to be obvious that if I deserve something, then I ought to receive it, and, furthermore, that if I deserve something, it is because of some property that I possess, something that I have done or something that I am. This property is the basis of desert. Given that considerations of desert determine who gets what, then it is clear that they will figure in debates about **distributive justice**. But this is where the controversy enters in. For, while it might seem that I deserve my riches because I have worked exceptionally hard for them, is it the case that I deserve the ability to work exceptionally hard? Perhaps this ability is itself just a product of the natural lottery, and distribution of talents under the natural lottery are, as **Rawls** memorably argued, 'arbitrary, from a moral point of view'. But if the capacity to get the property that is the basis of my desert claim is distributed in an arbitrary manner, then distribution according to desert only reinforces that original arbitrary distribution and so is ethically impermissible.

If desert does not 'go all the way down', but capacities for securing the bases of desert are distributed arbitrarily, then a distributive justice based on desert will itself be arbitrary, and we should look at other ways of distributing – perhaps in accordance with need.

Desert theorists react in a number of ways: they could argue that desert does indeed go all the way down, or that it goes down quite far enough to provide the basis for a distributive scheme. Or they might suggest that desert is a sufficiently primitive notion that, whatever the difficulties at the level of individual responsibility, it has to be incorporated into any notion of distributive justice that is to have rational consent.

See **distributive justice; Nozick, Robert**

Further reading: Pojman, L. P., and Pojman, O. M. (eds) 1999

difference-blind liberalism: The dominant account of political rules and institutions in much of the developed world has been a liberalism that claims to take persons as of equal value, ignoring morally irrelevant distinctions between them. This liberal account has provided a basis for opposition to legally instituted racism in South Africa and the southern states of the US. One way of thinking about this opposition to racist laws, such as those that made up the apartheid state, is to say that, from the point of view of justice, racial and cultural differences *don't matter*. To put it differently, Apartheid, Jim Crow Laws and so on are wrong because race doesn't count from a moral point of view: it is not morally relevant. Liberalism emphasises universal elements of our common humanity. These universal features of our existence provide the basis for saying that all are equal before the law. Religious and cultural differences exist, to be sure, but they are a private matter. In the political arena, we ought to be concerned with the common good and the **general will**.

See **multiculturalism**

Reading: Barry 2001; Baumeister 2000; Taylor 1995

difference principle: The difference principle is a key principle of distributive justice found in the work of **John Rawls,** and articulated in his *A Theory of Justice* (1971). The difference principle is the last of his principles concerning **distributive justice** and is lexically secondary to concerns about equal rights. Once all that has been dealt with, Rawls argues that the principles that would be chosen behind a **veil of ignorance** include the idea that inequalities are only justified in so far as they benefit the least well off. The idea is, first, that there is a presumption in favour of economic equality – **desert**-based inequalities are unjustified, because in the end they derive from the **natural lottery** – desert does not 'go all the way down'. But insisting on equalities that disadvantage the least well off seems absurd. Rather we should give priority to their interests and allow such exceptional inequalities.

The difference principle is controversial in many different ways: first, desert and entitlement theorists object to the way that desert is kept out of the distributive picture, and object to the perceived injustice of redistributive policies (see **Wilt Chamberlain**). Second, some egalitarians argue that Rawls licenses far too much inequality: the main category of exceptions is the practice of egalitarian tax regimes that would tax the talented very highly. These, it is said, would act as a disincentive for those people, which would damage the interest of the worst off, who would otherwise gain from the trickling down of benefits from the talented. But this – argue Rawls's critics – allows too much inequality to be justified by accepting the inegalitarian and selfish behaviour of the talented.

Finally, the scope of the difference principle is controversial. In *A Theory of Justice*, the difference principle applied within a single nation state – applying the difference principle internationally in a cosmopolitan way looks tricky in theory, because of the need to establish appropriate duties and responsibilities, and problematic in practice, necessitating difficult judgements about incentive effects and trickle down on a global scale.

See **distributive justice; Rawls, John**

Further reading: Pogge (ed.) 1989; Rawls 1971, 2001

dirty hands: The problem of involvement in politics – and, in particular, large-scale responsibility for others – raises the question of dirty hands – that political action may involve infringing upon everyday moral codes, deonto-logical prohibitions and/or human rights. The term was used by Jean Paul Sartre in his play *Les Mains sales*. However, an early discussion of the problem arises in **Machiavelli**'s *The Prince*, in which Machiavelli advises princes to dissimulate, and to practise cruelty, when the need arises.

The problem of dirty hands is dissolved if we adopt a simple **consequentialism**, according to which we need only to calculate the consequences of an action, and this will specify what constitutes a right action. It is then, simply, right to do whatever is conducive to the best con-sequences, and, having done the right thing, the sense of having dirty hands is a moral illusion. Arguably, though, this is the sort of moral view that has led to millions of lives being ended in the pursuit of some noble cause or other – and it is surely a difficulty that right action may involve huge and unjust sacrifices.

In contrast, squeamishness and an undue deference to ordinary moral rules may lead those in positions of responsibility to avoid taking tough decisions in difficult situations to secure public safety. It may be that political figures often face irresolvable moral dilemmas, in which the best outcome involves action that is wrong. Some have argued that, if this is the case, the mark of the moral agent is that she experiences remorse. In the end this seems to depend on the nature of the world in which we live: as Machiavelli puts it 'a prudent ruler cannot, and must not, honour his word when it places him at a disadvantage . . . If all men were good, this precept would not be good; but because men are wretched creatures who would not keep their word to you, you need not keep your word to them' (*The Prince*).

Further reading: Coady 1991; De Wijze 2004

discrimination: Very generally, discrimination takes place whenever one group of people is treated differently from another group of people. Of course, this happens all the time, and is not thought usually to involve an injustice. Architects discriminate between men and women when they plan separate changing facilities at swimming pools, and examiners discriminate between students when they give some high marks and some low marks. So the question arises – when is discrimination unjust? The answer seems to be when the discrimination is on the basis of some property that is not relevant to the justification of the practice. So if prizes were awarded only to the fastest white athletes in a race, this would amount to unjust discrimination, because, whilst being the fastest is relevant to getting a medal in a running race, being white is irrelevant within that contest. For discrimination to be unfair, it needs to diverge from an account of fairness, and so judgements about instances of unfair discrimination presuppose an account of justice, and particularly of distributive justice – of who gets what.

If someone is refused a job because of skin colour, that looks like unjust discrimination, but if they are refused a job because of a low level of academic achievement, then that looks more just, since the idea of distributing attractive jobs according to the academic qualifications of the job seekers seems reasonable, because of the link between the qualifications and their ability to do the job well.

There are three further qualifications. First, if the grounds of discrimination are irrelevant to the practice in question we ought to look at the contingent features of society to which they do relate. If they are relevant to deep-seated, long-lasting and acrimonious inequalities, then the discrimination looks more worrying than if the discrimination is on the basis of some free-floating eccentric discrinatory position such as a preference for rasberry ripple ice cream.

Secondly, the process of discrimination might not necessarily involve a conscious intention to discriminate, but might issue in discriminatory practices, nevertheless. It is contentious as to whether this is as bad an act as intentional discrimination.

Third, if discrimination on the basis of non-relevant criteria such as ethnicity is unjust, then what are we to make of policies that are designed to address injustice by means of such discrimination, except in an affirmative or positive way? These seem to fall under the same criteria, but some might argue that the conception of justice invoked here is too narrow, and that a wider conception of justice, pertaining to groups and institutions rather than individuals, is necessary.

Against the background of a general theory of justice, such as **luck egalitarianism**, what counts as fair and unfair discrimination becomes clear. Unfair discrimination is discrimination on the basis of what someone happens to be – the characteristics they bear purely by chance. Fair discrimination is discrimination on the basis of what people do, and so for what they can be held responsible. Discrimination, on this account, is one way of holding someone responsible.

However, there are problems even with this account. Is it unfair to discriminate against someone in the selection of a basketball team because they are, through no fault of their own, short And what about redressing imbalances shown to a group of individuals who have indeed been unfairly discriminated against in the past – is 'reverse discrimination' a legitimate option in these circumstances?

See **distributive justice; justice**
Further reading: Edmonds 2006

distributive justice: Area of political philosophy which is concerned with the distribution of assets, benefits, resources and things between individuals and groups of individuals. Generally distributive justice concerns who gets what, and principles of justice provide an answer to that question.

In predominantly free-market societies, who gets what is determined by the outcome of lots of small-scale trades, so that it might seem as if no overarching principle of justice is involved. But that would be a mistake – the overarching principle of justice is that 'who gets what ought to be determined by lots of small-scale trades' and it can be seen that this immediately conflicts with simple principles of justice – distribution according to **desert**, according to need, according to a priority granted to a particular group or according to some other pattern of distribution. What is distinctive about free-market distribution is not the absence of an underlying principle of justice but the absence of an agent that enforces the principle.

Debates over distributive justice have involved clashes between entitlement theories (proposed by Nozick and others) and Rawlsian theories of patterned distribution that give priority to the worst off. Others such as **Michael Walzer** have questioned the aim of generating general principles of distributive justice, arguing that the distribution of different resources ought to vary according to the social meaning of the resources concerned: distribution of health care, in one sphere, ought not to be determined by the same principles that determine the exchange of gifts between friends, for example. Others insist on the need to distinguish between choice and chance in the determination of distributive outcomes, asserting that redistribution ought to redress inequalities determined by chance, like the natural lottery, but not those that are an outcome of choice. Feminists and critical theorists such as **Iris Marion Young** have been critical of the 'distributive paradigm' – its focus on the distribution of things rather than identity constituting attitudes such as respect, and recent theorists of distributive justice such as Elizabeth Anderson have expressed concerns that luck-egalitarians miss the point about equality as a means to avoid oppression.

See **Aristotle; desert; entitlement theory; justice; Nozick, Robert; Rawls, John**

Further reading: Nozick 1974; Rawls 1971; Walzer 1983

divine right: A theory of authority explaining the legitimacy of a political order by reference to God's intentions or bequest. Sometimes this is the claim that rule is at God's command; sometimes the claim is that the monarch actually is a God. Divine right theorists argued that monarchs rule according to the will of God: their authority is not to be challenged, therefore, by earthly powers, and to question or challenge their authority is a way of questioning or challenging God's authority. Consequently, political dissent is a sort of heresy and political opposition is opposition to God's will. Divine right theories were specifically introduced by Augustus into the government of Rome in order to generate legitimacy for his absolute rule. Amongst those monarchs who championed divine right theories were James I of England and Louis XIV of France. Theorists of divine right included Sir Robert Filmer in *Patriarcha* (1680). Filmer argued for a divine role in the legitimacy of government in order to explain the fact of a political relation between the ruler and the ruled in the absence of, and pre-existing, any contractual relation.

Divine right theorists came under threat in the sixteenth century, and were subjected to withering polemical (and biblical) attack from **John Locke** in the little-read *First Treatise of Government*. As a claim to government authority divine right is now not a very effective or widespread claim, though it remains the preferred form of justification in a narrow set of cases, including that of the Dalai Lama in Tibet.

See **absolutism**

Further reading: Skinner 1978

division of labour: Process whereby the making of goods or the provision of services becomes increasingly fragmented into separate tasks performed by different individuals. There are two aspects to it: the extent to which individuals and families diverge from a model of self-sufficiency and the fine-grained division of labour in a modern manufacturing process. The social division of labour is discussed by Plato in *The Republic*. The division of labour in manufacturing is a mark of industrialisation and of technological change more generally, and Marxists argue that this change in the relations of production unleashes the productive forces for development. At the same time, the division of labour introduces further power relations into the productive process, since the individual labourer has less control over the process of production (and this leads to alienation) whilst his contribution is made more and more simple, so that labour becomes substitutable – that is, one unskilled labourer can easily be substituted for another. The process is sometimes described as de-skilling. According to critics it leads to **alienation** and makes it easier to drive down wages. In contrast, both the social and the manufacturing division of labour clearly contribute to speedier production, and the ability to produce much more complex artefacts that are beyond the capacity of a single labourer to produce. The increasing division of labour is also part of a change that leads to immense increases in production, with accompanying increases in general welfare. The relation between the costs and benefits of the division of labour is therefore complex. However, in market societies, as Adam Smith points out, the competitive drive towards the further dividing of labour often seems to sideline normative concerns.

See **alienation; capitalism**

Further reading: Marx 1844; Van Parijs 1995; Walzer 1983b

dystopia: The opposite of a Utopia – a dystopia is a model or vision of a world in which lives go badly. In political thought writers have conjured up dystopias in order to warn their readers of the dangers of certain particular social or political developments, or placed dystopia into their overarching model as a kind of hypothetical realisation of some aspect of human nature. Three different dystopic visions are **Hobbes**'s state of nature, Orwell's totalitarian picture in *1984* and Aldous Huxley's *Brave New World*.

Hobbes's state of nature was a hypothetical construct – a stark picture of a war of all against all, in which life was poor, nasty, brutish and short. Without a common power to keep us in check, the basest elements of our nature would resurface, and neither property nor life would be secure. Hobbes's dystopia is designed to give us a reason to defer to established authority.

Orwell's is designed to do the opposite. Characterising the incipient tendencies towards total control of individual's lives, Orwell imagines a society in which we are constantly watched by Big Brother, who directs our lives by way of a huge state bureaucratic machinery. There is some resistance to this domination, but the resistance is futile: Big Brother has the power to make us betray those we love and to believe that falsehoods are true.

Huxley's picture is different again, portraying a hierarchically divided society in which drugs and virtual interaction have taken the place of real interaction with particular human beings.

Each dystopic vision tells us something about the world in which we actually live, and provides us with warnings about our predicament: in this way, we can construct critical dystopias, just as we can construct critical utopias, such as **Rousseau**'s egalitarian participative democracy – as measuring sticks by which to evaluate our own societies.

See **state of nature**

Further reading: Hobbes 1996; Huxley 1932; Orwell 1949

$\boxed{\text{E}}$

entitlement theory: Name given to theories of **distributive justice** such as that of **Robert Nozick**, which are based on individual entitlements as the bedrock justification of who gets what. According to entitlement theories, there is a close moral relationship between me and mine, and that relationship is established according to some clear and simple moral rules: I am entitled to what I make with raw materials that I own, to what I buy in a fair exchange, to what is given to me on a voluntary basis, and so on. Nozick's slogan is modelled on the form of **Marx**'s slogan – from each according to ability, to each according to his need, but with radically different import – to each as he is entitled, from each as he voluntarily decides.

Certain thought experiments make the entitlement theory more persuasive: the experiment involving **Wilt Chamberlain** is thought to show that critics of the entitlement theory must seek to ban capitalist acts between consenting adults, and considerations about self ownership are designed to carry over intuitions about my control over my own body onto control over things that I make. At the heart of the entitlement theory is a modified form of **Locke**'s account and justification of the genesis of private property in the Second Treatise, which Nozick develops in order to found contemporary entitlements.

Critics of the entitlement theory ask whether it must be the case that entitlements have the absolute value that Nozick and others ascribe to them. Perhaps it is even the case that entitlements are a starting point, but do they really trump all other considerations (**infringement/ violation distinction**)? Others argue that the process of acquiring absolute entitlements is somewhat murky and suggest that it is unclear why other moral commitments, with equivalent intuitive support, fall by the wayside.

Overall, though Nozick's concern is to present a theory in which rights to our entitlements act as side constraints on public policy. The entitlement theory is not so much a theory of what policy ought to be adopted as one that circumscribes the areas in which public policy can operate: politics starts after my entitlements are respected.

See **eye lottery; Nozick, Robert; rights**
Further reading: Cohen, G. A. 1995; Nozick 1974

equality: For many political thinkers some form of equality is a fundamental virtue of a good society, but it is controversial over what sort of equality they have in mind. Equality is normally a scalar notion – it compares quantities: if I have five apples and you have five oranges we are equal in the number of fruit, but unequal in the numbers of oranges. So egalitarians have to answer two questions: why equality, and equality of what?

   Equality is thought to be a moral virtue because of the fundamental moral equality of persons. On this basis, what matters about an individual is that he is a single autonomous and rational being. To the extent that persons possess these basis properties they count, and they count for one. This egalitarianism dispenses with any notions of natural hierarchies in which those who are nobly born, or of a certain race, or men, or rich, have privileged access to social political and economic resources just because of these properties, which are arbitrary from the moral point of view.

   Political philosophers express this idea in different ways: utilitarians give evidence of some sort of commitment to equality when they insist that each life is to count for one in the utilitarian calculus, so that arbitrary privilege is eliminated. But critics of utilitarian thought insist that equal respect for persons creates constraints on treating them in some ways that a utilitarian would endorse – victimising the innocent, for example. Virtue theorists express a commitment to equality in consideration of human solidarity and unselfishness as virtues, but also often endorse the privileging of family and friends above strangers.

   The question of what is to be equalised is fraught with difficulties and very much hangs on the selection of measure. Separate entries will cover the main variants. The spectrum ranges from equality of external resources to 'mere' equality of respect. Equality of respect is (arguably) consistent with very widespread economic inequalities.

Criticisms of equality include its supposed conflict with political liberty and the supposed absurdity of 'levelling down'. Further, it is argued that equality would have damaging economic and social consequences. Finally, some have asserted that there are natural hierarchies, and that these ought to be reflected in just distributive arrangements.

See **capabilities approach; equality of opportunity; equality of resources; sufficiency**

Further reading: Anderson 1999; Clayton and Williams (eds) 2002; Dworkin 1981a; Dworkin 1981b; Frankfurt 1987; Williams [1969] 2005

equality of opportunity: Equality of opportunity is a principle which seems widely accepted in political thought, especially liberal political thought, but its precise meaning is sometimes unclear. For example, it enters into **Rawls**'s scheme as part of the first of the two principles of justice, lexically prior to the **difference principle,** and most liberal thinkers give it centre stage, often counterposing it to equality of outcome.

Equality of opportunity does not exist if some posts or roles are arbitrarily reserved for particular groups: the idea of equality of opportunity is that everyone may have a fair go at attaining a particular goal. Thus religious restrictions on civil service jobs, racial restrictions on university entrance, and gender restrictions on sporting activities and so on, all seem to infringe a concern with equal opportunities. The image that those who draw a strong contrast between equality of opportunity and equality of outcome have in mind is that of a running race in which all start at the same point, and have an equal opportunity to win the race, but where the outcome is varied, according to who performs best.

Critics of equality of opportunity argue, variously, that this account of equality is substantially meaningless. Morally arbitrary genetic factors help to determine who wins a running race, just as morally arbitrary social backgrounds help to determine who get the top jobs, places at university and income and privileges. Equality of opportunity, they say, simply gives a liberal gloss to wide-ranging and unjust inequalities. Rather more sophisticated accounts, such as those of luck-egalitarians aim to equalise between individuals to the extent that outcomes are a result of luck, and allow inequalities to the extent that they are a result of the choices of the individuals concerned.

Other critics, including multiculturalists, suggest that 'opportunity' is a subject-dependent concept – that cultural and other resources are necessary for individuals really to take advantage of the opportunities that appear to face them.

See **equality; equality of resources; justice**
Further reading: Rawls 1971

equality of resources: If individuals are equally worthy of respect, and that respect applies to the projects that constitute their lives, then it might appear that individuals are entitled to an equal share of the earth's resources. Portioning up the bundles of resources in this way might be time consuming, but it might look like the most just solution to the problem of **distributive justice**.

Equality of resources, however, faces several powerful objections. First, since individual's needs are not equal, a pattern of equality of resources will diverge from the pattern needed to secure equal satisfaction of needs or preferences: the able bodied will gain at the expense of the unable, and those with more expensive tastes will not be able to meet them. Equality of resources will mean unequal levels of welfare. Equality of resources also seems to conflict markedly with intuitions about **desert** and responsibility. If we insist on equality with respect to desert, it seems right that those who deserve more get more. Perhaps those who are responsible for generating more resources are entitled to a larger share.

If the link between patterns of distribution and individual contribution is broken – as equality of resources suggests, then there will be a disincentive on individual contributions. If these fall, there will be less of the cake to go around, so that equal shares will be smaller shares.

These objections come from those who are concerned with securing distributive equality, but think that equality of resources measures the wrong thing. But equality of resources is also open to the criticisms that apply to patterns of distributive justice more generally – that it seems to infringe self-ownership rights, that it also seems to imply constant intervention by the redistributive agency, and so on.

See **capabilities approach; desert; entitlement theory; equality; justice; sufficiency**

Further reading: Dworkin 1981a

equality of welfare: In response to criticisms of the notion of equality of resources, many egalitarian thinkers have articulated a commitment to equality of welfare as an alternative measure for securing **distributive justice**. Generally the welfare criterion refers to the idea of a life that goes well, that flourishes, fulfils its potential and so on, but in welfare economics the idea is rather more shallow – and more measurable – the satisfaction of preferences.

The advantages of welfare equality over resource equality is that it seems better to meet the objection that individuals have different projects, and different resource requirements. But the view is still subject to criticisms – especially that it endorses a distortion of distribution patterns towards those who have expensive tastes. If I can only really enjoy expensive champagne and caviar – all other food tastes dusty and bland – while my neighbour has more mundane culinary preferences, then equalising our welfare will mean shifting the distribution of resources towards me in a way that seems unjust.

Some advocates of welfare equality (such as Sen) respond to this objection by attempting to objectify welfare away from an account of subjective preference satisfaction towards an account based on objective lists of capabilities which are generally conducive to a good life. This account tends to avoid the problem of expensive tastes, but runs the risk of invoking a rather arbitrary and essentialist account of what constitutes a good life.

See **equality; equality of resources; justice**

Further reading: Clayton and Williams 2002; Dworkin 1981b; Sen 1995

essential/accidental distinction: This distinction, which comes from **Aristotle**, allows us to group the properties of a thing which it must have in order to be that thing, and the properties which it need not have. It is essential to a person being that person that they have the parents that they have: it is not essential that they live in the particular place where they happen to live. 'Accidental' here, does not convey the idea of unintendedness that it usually has.

In political philosophy, one of the key disagreements is over which of the properties of human nature are essential and which are accidental, and so potentially specific to a space and time. **Hobbes** wanted to show that self-interested behaviour is essential: Marxists and Anarchists want to insist that such behaviour is 'accidental' and therefore potentially eliminable.

See **Aristotle; state of nature**

Further reading: Macpherson 1962

express consent: Express consent is consent given explicitly by a promise to obey the government and laws of a state. An example of express consent is the ceremony which naturalised citizens of the USA and the UK undergo when they become such citizens.

In attempting to answer the question 'why should someone obey the law?', consent theorists often start by outlining an unproblematic case – express consent – where the obligation to obey the law comes directly from a written or spoken agreement to do so. This consent or agreement is, then, given expressly or explicitly. It is just like a promise to obey the state, and promises generate obligations in a relatively straightforward way.

Citizenship rituals often involve something like express consent. When immigrants to a nation state declare formal allegiance to that state, or when citizens publicly declare their loyalty to the state, then it seems straightforward to suggest that they thereby undertake an obligation to obey the laws. Express consent therefore functions at the core of theories of social contract that aim to explain the normative basis of the state.

However, if express consent is the key to political obligation, then all modern states will face problems. First, the consent that can be given can also be withdrawn. Second, many individuals do not have the opportunity to give their express consent. Third, it seems unlikely that, but for a very few, states were founded on any such expression of consent. This suggests that almost all hitherto existing states can be considered as illegitimate. For this reason, theorists who aim to set political obligation on a contractual basis tend to favour some form of **tacit consent** as a way of understanding the obligation to obey the state. But this runs into problems too, since the conditions of tacit consent do not seem to map across to the more straightforward case of express consent. For example, on some accounts of tacit consent, I can give my consent without knowing that I do so.

Nevertheless, express consent is certainly an important element in any position designed to secure general political obligation, though it is likely now to figure more as part of a mixed strategy of arguments for such a position.

See **consent**

Further reading: Nozick 1974

expressive freedom: The freedom to express views, to articulate opinions, to publish words and pictures, that is standard in liberal conceptions of justice. However, the feminist lawyer Catharine Mackinnon outlines the ways a commitment to equality (such as in the US 14th Amendment) might be something against which unfettered freedom of expression ought to give way.

Mackinnon brings together a number of different arguments about the relationship between pornography, hate speech and freedom of speech. She argues that 'the law is insensitive to the damage done to social equality by expressive means'. This idea that expressive means can undermine equality seems to contradict the old saying: 'sticks and stones may break my bones, but words can never hurt me'. It suggests that, by their effect on me and on others, words and images can threaten my position, restrict my freedom and, in particular, place me in relations of domination and subservience to others – some expressive acts undermine relations of equality between people as individuals and as groups.

See **toleration**
Further reading: Mackinnon 1993

eye lottery: This is a thought experiment designed to highlight some issues in the discussion of **distributive justice**.

Suppose a significant minority of the population of a country are born without eyes. However, medical procedures exist which allow for the generally successful transplantation of eyes from those with two to those with none. This worsens the position of those donors who have two eyes, but improves the position of the eyeless. Suppose, too that the improvement in the position of those who receive an eye is much greater than the loss to those who lose an eye. There is a lottery, which selects at random those who have two eyes, and they are required – forced, if necessary – by the state to undergo the operation to give up an eye for transplantation.

The eye lottery is designed to be repugnant. However, some opponents of redistributive taxation regard it as relevantly analogous to redistributive taxation, and argue that the condemnation of the eye lottery ought to carry over into condemnation of schemes of redistributive taxation. They say that the eye lottery models intuitions about self-ownership rights and about infringements on autonomy, which speak also against taxation to help the needy.

Advocates of redistributive taxation could bite the bullet, accepting that there are no moral differences between the eye lottery and redistributive taxation but argue that there is nothing wrong with the eye lottery. They would then advocate a retraining of our moral intuitions so that we did not find the thought of the eye lottery repugnant. Alternatively, and more plausibly, proponents of redistributive taxation could endorse moral opposition to the eye lottery but deny its relevance to the case of

redistributive taxation by citing morally relevant differences between the two.

See **distributive justice; Nozick, Robert; self-ownership**
Further reading: Wolff 1991

F

fairness, principle of: The principle of fairness was first for-
mulated by the legal philosopher H. L. A. Hart in 1955:
'When a number of persons conduct any joint enterprise
according to rules and thus restrict their liberty, those
who have submitted to these restrictions when required
have a right to a similar submission from those who have
benefited by their submission' (p. 185). **Rawls** formulates
a similar principle – that when people engage in a cooperative project, and their engagement restricts their
liberty, 'those who have submitted to these restrictions
have a right to a similar acquiescence on the part of those
who have benefited from their submission' (1971: 95).

The principle is designed to answer the problem of
political obligation, by showing that non co-operators
have an obligation to go along with the project. But it is
not obvious why this should be the case. **Nozick** (1974:
93) famously cites a thought experiment in which a
public address system is set up, and operated by members
of the neighbourhood, once a day each year – there are
365 people in this neighbourhood. Although a person
clearly benefits from the public address system which
broadcasts music, interesting talks and so on – there is no
obligation that arises from the fact of its existence as a cooperative project. This criticism generally points to the
need for consent in the generation of obligations.

See **free rider problem; Nozick, Robert**
Further reading: Hart 1955; Klosko 1992; Nozick 1974

false consciousness: Term drawn from Marx to describe the situation in which individuals or classes are systematically unaware of, or misunderstand, their own interests, or, more generally, misperceive the nature of the world in which they live, or are subject to collective self-deception. Critical to the idea of false consciousness is an account of systematic, not haphazard, misperception, and an attempt to explain this misperception in terms of material relations in the world. So, for example, belief in God is a form of false consciousness, first because there is no God, but, second, because the belief that there is a God is systematically produced, because of its capacity to provide consolation in an inhuman world. As well as being the opium of the masses, religion is also 'the sigh of the oppressed creature'('Critique of Hegel's Philosophy of Right', in Marx 1994).

Some feminists have revived **Marx**'s use to suggest that women who claim to be happy and fulfilled in a homemaking role are exhibiting a form of false consciousness.

False consciousness seems often to be explained functionally. It arises because it is good or functional for some purpose (like the maintenance of elite power). Possibly there is a conspiracy to keep us dumb. But functional explanations are highly contested, and good ones require an account of the micro-stories that might underlie them. But often these stories take the form of conspiracies, and the evidence for such conspiracies is very often meagre.

False consciousness seems to rest on a fairly specific account of true interests, and corresponding true consciousness. But the error theory is only as necessary as the account of true interests is secure. In the absence of a generally fixed and secure account of true interests, the claim that individuals are 'falsely conscious' sometimes sounds like a charge made in bad faith.

Further reading: Rosen 2000

fascism: Name given to a social and political movement of the early half of the twentieth century. Fascism is named after the *fasci* – or bundles of sticks which represented the idea of strength through unity, originating from Ancient Rome. Fascism drew on several disparate ideas: ideas of radical nationalism, Nietzchean accounts of the 'will to power' and the cult of a leader, Freudian critiques of rationality, and the notion of a third way to capitalism and communism. A central component of most fascist thought was the importance of the corporate state driven on by a dominant, strong leader. Racist ideas, sometimes with a biological basis, are found in some varieties of fascism, but are less apparent in others. In each expression of fascism these components were expressed more or less, and in different combinations – for example, Mussolini's fascism was not as essentially anti-semitic as Nazism. Perhaps the clearest common element was the idea, as Roger Eatwell puts it, of fascism as a *holistic–national–radical–Third Way*. Amongst philosophical precursors were Nietzche and Georges Sorel, though in different ways. Amongst supporters were Martin Heidegger and, briefly, Carl Schmitt.

Further reading: Eatwell 2003

feminism: Feminism in political philosophy involves a commitment to the equality of women, or, in more radical forms, the emancipation of women. What that equality means is subject to wide differentiation. **Wollstonecraft**'s *Vindication of the Rights of Woman* (1792) is an early tract arguing for women's participation in public life and espousing (against **Rousseau**) the view that women and men are essentially the same and equally rational. Since the argument of political participation rests on rationality, women ought to have equal rights.

The *locus classicus* for equal rights feminism is **Mill**'s and Harriet Taylor's *The Subjection of Women*. This work is parsimonious in its assumptions about essential natures, simply arguing for legal equality as a default position, rather than engaging in a refutation of essentialist claims about male superiority.

Socialist feminism contrasts with liberal feminism in that it locates the causes of women's oppression not in legal disparities but in economic structures of domination and subordination. Consequently it locates the potential for women's emancipation and equal treatment in the overcoming of those economic relations, rather than in reform at a strictly legal level.

Radical feminism shifts the focus again to the level of discourse and ideology rather than legal rights or economic structures: its key concept is **patriarchy**, and many radical feminists lay an emphasis on the criticism of aspects of patriarchal culture, such as pornography.

Contemporary feminists often distance themselves from **difference-blind liberalism**, attacking it from the perspective of critical theory. One example is **Iris Marion Young,** who argues that the raising of an abstract and universal model of political participation in fact ignores difference and so undermines the position of women and minorities. In fact, Young argues, genuine equality demands special group rights.

However, for some critics, this can seem to reduce claims that seem to be just because of their justification by universal principles into special pleading.

See **authority/authoritarianism; patriarchy**

Further reading: Okin 1991; Pateman 1988; Young 1990

Foucault, Michel (1926–84): Foucault was a French theorist and philosopher of power, discourse and sexuality. Foucault's influence has been strong in the social sciences, and he has directed a critical view towards various social institutions, including prisons, medicine, psychiatry and sexuality. However, he is a more minor figure in philosophy as such. Foucault worked within no philosophical system, nor did he articulate a coherent vision of the nature of philosophical work or its aim or content.

His thought is often characterised as postmodern, though this is a label he himself rejected. He is known for his study of discourse and the relationships between knowledge and power. Foucauldian approaches take a social constructivist form, in opposition to an allegedly oversimple view of truth and explanation as the correspondence between an independent social reality and our understanding of it.

See **postmodernism**

Further reading Gutting 2005

foundationalism: The idea that knowledge has secure and indubitable foundations and that, from these foundations, a system of secure beliefs can be constructed. Standardly, the source of secure foundations is thought to be empirical knowledge, derived from sense experience. Conceived of as a crude image, foundationalisim is subject to serious criticism: are our senses indubitable? What are the best ways of constructing knowledge – must it rely on empirical foundations? Are not some truths about the world the product of social construction?

Nevertheless, anti-foundationalist criticism can also give rise to the abandonment of any criteria by which to judge knowledge claims, with disastrous results.

See **contextualism; postmodernism**

Further reading: Boghossian 2006

Frankfurt School: An influential group of European Marxists, many of them Jewish, which was formed as the Institute for Social Research at the University of Frankfurt in 1923 and then took refuge from the Nazis in the USA, forming the New School for Social Research in New York. Key figures were Walter Benjamin, Max Horkheimer and Theodore Adorno; later adherents include Herbert Marcuse and Jürgen Habermas. Their overall approach was anti-reductionist and looked critically at the economic determinism thought to characterise the West European communist parties in the interwar period. Frankfurt School theorists were more likely to take cultural texts as their starting point and their aesthetic focus was a strong contrast with the economism of the official movement. More radical still was their take on the Enlightenment and its universalist and foundational traditions. Frankfurt School theorists tend to reject the idea that science can be value free – thus rejecting the scientistic and positivist aspirations of much official **Marxism**. Rather, they seek to pursue a critical theory, which is explicitly committed from the beginning. The Frankfurt School emphasise the role of consciousness in historical change. Critical theory is at its most penetrating in *Dialectic of Enlightenment* (Horkheimer and Adorno [1947] 2002) which shows some ways in which the technophile and rational bureaucracy of Nazi Germany was able to perpetuate the Holocaust: scientific rationality did not prove an obstacle to evil – rather, it enabled evil to triumph.

Thinking in the Frankfurt tradition is still evident, though increasingly critical theory finds common cause with the anti-foundational and self-reflexive and culturally focused elements in postmodernism.

See **deliberative democracy; false consciousncess; Marxism; Habermas, Jürgen; postmodernism**

Further reading: Geuss 1981

free rider problem: Name for a puzzle in both normative political philosophy and in political analysis and policy formation. Suppose an individual jumps on a bus into town, but both does not pay and is not caught by the conductor. What is wrong with this action, and what ought to be done about it?

Perhaps it is thought that the action is not universalisable – if everyone refused to pay, the collective good of the bus service would disappear. But free rider problems emerge precisely when others do pay – the free rider is parasitic on the paying riders. But further, the free rider does not directly harm any one else: the bus service would run without him, and his action does not diminish the amount of the good available for anyone else.

For some (such as H. L. A. Hart), the free rider problems suggest something like the principle of **fairness** – that if I receive some gain from a collective enterprise that others contribute to then, in fairness, I ought to contribute to that collective effort. The fairness principle seems to capture an ideal of community solidarity, and the intertwining of people's lives which acts as a normative standard for criticism of free riding. In contrast, **Nozick** and other libertarians argue that, if a good is not solicited in someway, then there is precisely no obligation to contribute to its supply.

Free rider problems crop up across the series of problems with which political philosophers concern themselves, wherever collective goods or collective action is susceptible to disruption by individuals who can make low-cost gains: the non-union worker who refuses to strike but takes the ensuing pay rise, the tax evader who uses public services, the cyclist who tucks in behind the bunch before winning the final sprint. In all these cases there is a question of unfairness, and the opportunity to explore strategic and normative solutions, including the development of a group ethos against cheating, honour amongst thieves, the ethics of the peloton, or union traditions of solidarity. Sometimes these will involve *post hoc* sanctions taken against the free rider. Nevertheless, these problems remain intractable.

See **fairness, principle of; prisoner's dilemma**

Further reading: Cullity 1995; Gauthier 1986; Hart 1955

functionalism: Functionalism is a form of explanation in the social sciences that figures in understandings of social and historical change put forward by Marxists and others. Suppose that I wish to hang a picture in my living room. In order to do this, I need to put a screw in the wall, which requires using a screwdriver. So I take a screwdriver to the living room. Suppose I am asked, 'Why is the screwdriver in the living room?' It would be true (although more than a little odd) for me to answer that 'the screwdriver is in the living room because it functions in the task of hanging pictures; its being in the living room helps to satisfy the need for hanging pictures'. The *function* of the screwdriver – the fact that it is good at doing something that needs to be done – *explains* its spatio-temporal location. This is the general form of functional explanations – the function of an institution, activity and so on is what explains its existence.

What, though, was odd about the answer above? It was that the explanation made no reference to my deciding to hang a picture and fetching the screwdriver. It would be much more straightforward to say that the screwdriver is in the living room because 'I fetched it to hang the picture.'

The functional benefits of the screwdriver are explanatory, but only indirectly – only through my desire to hang a picture and my belief that a screwdriver would be good for doing the job. I enter into the story as a purposive agent, and it is by acting on the screwdriver that I bring it about that the functional explanation is true. To say that 'the screwdriver is in the living room because it is functional for the task of hanging pictures' seems to suggest something that is not true: that it got there on its own. But there was an obvious mechanism by which the screwdriver came into the living room.

See **analytical Marxism; historical materialism; Marxism; methodological individualism**

Further reading: Cohen, G. A. 1978; Cohen, G. A. 1982; Elster 1982; Elster 1985

G

game theory: Game theory looks at human interaction in a variety of formal ways to show up the mutual interdependence of our actions and the way that rational actions might have consequences quite different from those intended by the actor.

See **assurance game; prisoner's dilemma; zero–sum game**
Further Reading: Hampton 1986

general will: Term most associated with **Rousseau** and his canonical work: the Social Contract. The general will is the key category of Rousseau's thought. Political society, rather than being an assemblage of the separate and individual concerns of individuals, brings into place a new phenomenon – the general will. This refers to what is, objectively, in all our interests taken as a whole. It is the duty of a citizen to seek out and obey the general will, and the best way to do this is usually to vote. But the voting must be entered into in the right spirit – as individuals genuinely seek to understand and support what is in the best interests of the social whole. For Rousseau, the general will cannot err, but we can err in trying to discover what it is. Once the general will is established, however, the question of political obligation is resolved. This problem, which arose from the appearance that to obey political authority is a denial of **autonomy**, is removed if we understand that in obeying the general will we are only obeying ourselves. Those who do not act according to the general will ought to be forced to do so, thinks Rousseau, though this only amounts to forcing them to be free.

The idea of a general will is present in **Hegel** and the notion of acting for the common good is found in the later British Idealists such as T. H. Green and Bernard Bosanquet. **Berlin** and other liberal pluralists are sceptical of the notion of the general will and regard it as potentially coercive, and the bluntness of Rousseau's prescriptions now seem disfavoured. However, there are more liberal and egalitarian readings of Rousseau, according to which the generality of the general will is an obstacle against the unjust picking out of, for example, groups defined ethnically or by sex.

See **Rousseau, Jean-Jacques**

Further reading: Bertram 2003; Dent 2005

globalisation: Globalisation – which can be glossed as the phenomenon of increasing interconnectedness across the globe – has become of great importance in the last two decades. The collapse of the Soviet Union and its associated states as well as the rapid development of communication technologies has led to the growth of a global village. The impact of this phenomenon on positions taken within political philosophy is complex: some see globalisation as providing a basis for the emergence of a cosmopolitan governing order, and a cosmopolitan conception of justice. Part of the institutional structure that is relevant here is the International Criminal Court. Critics of globalisation see it as the expansion of specifically US and specifically capitalist hegemony over much of the world, bringing with it widespread exploitation and increasing global inequality, and cultural imperialism. The truth is more complicated – though undoubtedly changing communication technologies have transformed and in some cases undermined national identities

See **cosmopolitanism; nationality**

Green political philosophy: A concern with other creatures is not a wholly new feature of political thought, but a serious engagement with issues concerning our obligations to the environment is a recent phenomenon, at least within the Western tradition.

This concern has been motivated by a new understanding of our obligations to future generations and a less anthropocentric understanding of what counts for moral consideration. This second phenomenon has led to a widening of the 'circle of concern' from human beings to other species, of sentient creatures, to plants and finally to the overall environment itself – mountains, rivers, the rain forests and so on.

A widening of the circle of concern raises the question why we should concern ourselves with such things. There are two views: the first is that our non-human surroundings are of moral value in themselves; the second is that our non-human surroundings are of value because of the moral value they generate in human beings. The difference between these positions can be brought out by considering 'last man' arguments. Suppose the last man on earth, who is himself about to perish, takes a flame thrower to some plants – perhaps rare and beautiful ones. Would he have committed a moral wrong? Some 'intrinsic value' theorists would be committed to saying yes, even though (*ex hypothesi*) no harm was done to human interests, no human needs went unmet.

The distinction between intrinsic and instrumental valuation of the moral worth of the environment gives rise to a distinction between 'deep' and 'shallow' green theories: the terms originate from Arne Naess. Shallow environmentalism derives concern for the environment from concern about human beings. Deep environmentalism involves what Ness terms 'the equal right to live and blossom' of all forms of life – a commitment to equal rights sometimes known as biospheric egalitarianism. This is sometimes thought to be open to the objection that the smallpox virus ought not to be attributed the same rights as less harmful forms of life.

See **anthropocentrism**

Further reading: Carter 1999; Naess 1989

Habermas, Jürgen (1929–): German philosopher and sociologist, a student of Theodore Adorno. Habermas can perhaps be thought of as a second generation member of the **Frankfurt School**, particularly in his earlier career. But this was a two-edged legacy: Habermas took on the Marxist influence of the Frankfurt school particularly in his work on the 'legitamation crisis' of the late twentieth century: political legitimacy rather than production was the site of the Marxist theory of crisis. In other theoretical work Habermas looks for a unity of rationally acceptable emancipatory discourses that can transcend academic specialisation and theoretical relativism

In *The Theory of Communicative Action* ([1981] 1984) Habermas outlines the idea of an 'ideal speech-situation' in which progress can be made towards the truth by means of rational argumentation under conditions of autonomy. The speech act account of criteria for truth gives rise to discussion of and endorsement of some form of deliberative democracy in Habermas's work. This is further extended in his major work *Between Facts and Norms* (1996) and within his debate with **Rawls** over the development of Rawls's views into political liberalism.

See **autonomy; deliberative democracy; Frankfurt school**
Further reading: Habermas 1986; Habermas 1996

harm principle: Anti-paternalist principle of J. S. Mill. The principle states that the only purpose for which we may intervene in the action of another against their will is to prevent harm to others. Such harm is a necessary (though not a sufficient) condition of intervention. Those actions that do not affect others – self-regarding actions – may not be prohibited. The principle therefore respects individual autonomy. For example, it lies behind the view that any sort of consenting sexual acts between adults ought to be allowed. Some version of the harm principle is central to **liberalism,** because it defines a limit for the state against the autonomous individual.

Mill's principle is that intervention into our lives is only ever justifiable if our actions are causing, or likely to cause, harm to others. Harm to others is the test – the threshold that must be passed, if there is to be any discussion about whether the state should intervene. The principle is more restrictive than it might at first appear. It does not say that the state should intervene whenever others are harmed; some sorts of harm to others might still be permitted. It is a negative principle, arguing that when there is no harm to others there is no question of intervention. It looks like an anti-paternalist dictum: we should not interfere with people's lives in order to save them from themselves.

But the 'one simple principle' only starts the ball rolling: it outlines a set of actions – those that are 'self-regarding' in which the government has no legitimate interest. But are there any such actions? Is the set of actions that are self-regarding an empty one? If there are no self-regarding actions, the principle is empty.

For Mill, the principle is justified by its contribution to overall utility, and this connection is contentious: are autonomous individuals necessarily happier than less autonomous ones? Critics have also asked what is to count as harm. If 'mere offence' (such as the offence caused by unusual consenting sex) is to be excluded, why is this?

See **autonomy; liberalism; Mill, John Stuart; utilitarianism**.

Further reading: Raz 1986

Hayek, Friedrich August von (1899–1992): Hayek was primarily an economist, but has made a significant contribution to political philosophy as well. Perhaps best known for his condemnation of state planning as 'the road to serfdom' Hayek claims that capitalism is the best bulwark against tyranny. This is partly because of an epistemological point – reason and information processing abilities are limited, and the workings of a complex industrial or post-industrial society are simply unknowable both in practice and in principle. Decisions taken by agents within the economy, including the agency of the state, generate outcomes, but those outcomes are unknowable in advance. Rather than attempting to intervene within the market – an approach that has a political and social dynamic to ever more intervention – the state should restrain itself, and let the free flow of information that is generated by free markets become more general.

The claim that the more free the market, the stronger are liberal rights, looks both contingent, and sometimes false. Scandinavian social democracies evidence both high levels of state intervention and strong civil liberties, whilst some neo-liberal experiments have been accompanied by political repression.

See **capitalism; liberalism; libertarianism; Nozick, Robert**

Further reading: Gray1986; Hayek 1944; Hayek1988

Hegel, G. W. F. (1770–1831): German idealist political philosopher, who revolutionised political philosophy, laid down some tracks along which **Marx** would follow, and established idealism as an essential part of the canon.

Hegel's system derives from the theory of the dialectic – a complex process that essentially involves the increasing determination of an undifferentiated subject through processes of negation and conflict. This is the root to knowledge – as the concept becomes increasingly determinate, it also becomes knowable. However, this process is delayed – the 'Owl of Minerva spreads its wings only at dusk' (that is, wisdom can only be gained in retrospect [Hegel (1820) 1991]). The process of the dialectic is not only a process of pure thought. Because 'what is real is rational' it is also – as the term idealism suggests – the structuring principle of the world.

Hegel's political philosophy is found in *The Philosophy of Right* – a difficult work, but one with many insights on property, freedom, alienation, the family and the state. For Hegel, private property is a condition of freedom, the family is a paradigm of non-contractual allegiance (and marital love exemplifies the dialectical emergence of a subject that is a 'we'). For Hegel, the state is the highest manifestation of freedom which arises from the transcendence of the family and civil society – neither the particularity of the family nor the atomisation of civil society really match up to the fully realised free individual in the state.

After Hegel's death, his supporters split into Right and Left Hegelians – the former emphasised his foregrounding of the obligations to the state, the latter emphasising his account of alienation and the master–slave dialectic. **Marx**'s own contribution was only made possible by Hegel.

See **alienation; Marx, Karl; property**
Further reading: Knowles 2002; Taylor 1975

historical materialism: Name given to the approach to history of **Karl Marx** and later Marxists, but not used by Marx himself to describe his method. **Historical materialism** also refers to a rather codified and formulaic doctrine associated with the Communist Party of the Soviet Union, and twinned with dialectical materialism in the *History of the Soviet Union (Short Course)*. It is difficult to separate the ideas of Marx from their later codification, but it is worth the attempt. Marx's view is expressed in an early version in Part 1 of the *German Ideology*, and has its most succinct codification in the 1859 *Preface to a Contribution to a Critique of Political Economy*. In that text Marx claims that the productive forces, which develop though technical change, are first encouraged then constrained by the productive relations that cover them. When the strain becomes too much, a revolutionary overthrow of the productive relations takes place. This ushers in a new set of productive relations under which the productive forces can begin to develop again.

An influential recent interpretation – that of **G. A. Cohen** has it that the relation between productive relations and productive forces is functional – that the relations take the form they do because thereby they encourage the development of the forces of production, and this functional account has been the target of criticism. More generally, Marx's account is thought by some critics to be overly reductionist, missing out the many and varied sources of historical change and reducing them to economic and technological changes. Moreover, however useful Marx's account has been in analysing historical changes, it has not had a happy record at successful prediction.

Further reading: Cohen, G. A. 1978

Hobbes, Thomas (1588–1679): An English philosopher whose major work in political philosophy is *Leviathan* (1651). Other important works include *De Cive* (1642) and *The Elements of Law* (1640). *Leviathan* provides a justification of near-absolute authority based not on a natural hierarchy but on a materialist and mechanical account of humankind. Hobbes's concern is not to show that everyone is fundamentally selfish, but that when everything is permitted (by the 'right of nature') the ensuing uncertainty, and the actions of a vain-glorious minority justify pre-emptive action. Understanding human beings in this way, Hobbes considers that life without a social authority would be appalling. Life in this hypothetical **state of nature** would famously be 'poor, nasty, brutish and short'. Recognising this, men ought to assent to a common power, and transfer their rights to that sovereign power, once and for all. They ought to recognise and obey the 'laws of nature', which are, amongst other things, guidelines for peaceful existence. This sort of reasoning, Hobbes argues, combines prudence with morality. On this view, morality is a construction of rational individuals pursuing their own interests. The authority of the sovereign is only nearly, not fully, absolute, because it does not include the power to make an individual complicit in their own death: the authority of the state is derived from the authority of the individual over themselves, and there are limits to how far this can be transferred to a sovereign. In this way and others, such as the use of the device of the **social contract**, and the attempt to provide a rational justification of state power, Hobbes is a precursor of the liberal tradition, and he provides a foil for that tradition, most notably **Locke**. However, his position is also congenial to **conservatism**, since it prescribes obedience to existing authority.

See **absolutism; political obligation; right of nature; social contract; state of nature**

Further reading: Gauthier 1977; Gauthier 1986; Hampton 1986

Hohfeld, Werner (1879–1918): American jurist and philosopher of law, best known for his analytical account of rights *Fundamental Legal Conceptions as Applied in Judicial Reasoning*, published in 1919, in which he shows that **rights** are correlatives of duties. For Hohfeld this is not a substantive claim (unlike the claim of some political communitarians today that 'we should concentrate more on responsibilities than rights') but an analytical claim about the meaning of words. If X has a right to A then others have a duty towards X (not to interfere with X's getting or doing A). This sense of a right meaning a correlative duty is the key to Hohfeld's thought. However, he also wanted to break down the notion of a right into particular components. There were four kinds of rights and four kinds of duties. Rights break down into claim-right, privilege, power and immunity, and each has correlates: duty, no-right, liability and disability.

In his analysis, Hohfeld distinguishes, for example, between a 'claim-right' and a 'power'. A claim-right on the part of X requires a duty on the part of Y, but a power, the ability of X to do something (vis-à-vis Y), requires a liability on the part of Y. Hohfeld stipulated the opposites (not correlates) of the four key rights claim-right, privilege, power and immunity as not-claim-right, duty, disability and liability. Hohfeld's analysis is the subject of ongoing philosophical argument, over what exactly the relations of correlativity involve. But it has proved influential in the study of both legal and moral rights, because it prescribes a generally helpful analytical programme. Each ordinary language right – such as the right to private property – can be unravelled into a nest of relationships – claim-rights and powers, immunities and privileges. Justifying a right becomes a much more complicated business, in some ways easier – since sometimes it is simply a matter of denying that X has a duty not to do whatever it is he is supposed to have a claim-right to do. At other times, it is much more than this, but the notion of a full right can be built up from these analytical foundations. Certainly, Hohfeld's analysis is important to much contemporary work in political philosophy, such as the arguments for left-libertarianism, which endorse self-ownership rights but deny that these rights entail endorsing absolute rights over property. This disaggregative approach to property rights relies on something like Hohfeld's account.

See **rights**

Further reading: Steiner 1994; Wenar 2005

Hume, David (1711–76): Perhaps the most important philosopher of the eighteenth century. Hume's contribution to political philosophy is fertile, though unsystematic. In his essay *Of the Original Contract*, Hume criticises those such as **Locke** who explain our allegiance to a political society in terms of a contract. Hume's critique is at least in part historical, but also contains a famous thought experiment in which he compares residence in a country to remaining on a ship. In neither case, he suggests, can legitimate authority be deduced from the fact that the individual remains in the same place: tacit consent does not justify political obedience. In contrast, he argues that the only justification for obedience is derived from utility, so laying the basis for the defences of **utilitarianism** from **Bentham** and **Mill**.

Hume provides a utilitarian defence of private property and private rights, necessary, he thinks, for justice. In *An Enquiry Concerning the Principles of Morals* he outlines the **circumstances of justice** in an account which is the locus classicus of contemporary discussion. Hume was a Tory, and adopted a sceptical approach to political matters: his preferred constitution was for a mixed republican and monarchic system, for which Great Britain was the model.

See **Circumstances of Justice**
Further reading: Miller 1981

I

income rights see **control/income rights**

infringement/violation distinction: Distinction drawn by Judith Jarvis Thomson between two ways in which someone's **rights** may be affected. If someone has a right that p, and p is made false, then their right that p is infringed. However, it is only violated if the act of making p false was wrong. The distinction therefore means that it is possible to infringe someone's rights without acting wrongly – so it is possible to infringe but not violate someone's rights. The distinction is denied by advocates of absolute rights such as **Nozick**.

See **deontology; entitlement theory; Nozick, Robert; rights**
Further reading: Thomson 1990

interest theory of rights: Version of a rights-founding theory that founds **rights** on vital interests – as the political philosopher Joseph Raz puts it: 'X has a right if and only if X can have rights and, other things being equal, an aspect of X's well-being (his interest) is a sufficient reason for holding some other person(s) to be under a duty' (Raz 1986: 166).

The interest theory does seem to cope well with the problem of unwaivable rights and it allows the ascription of rights to incompetents.

However, it does not fit with other common considerations about rights. It seems that it is possible for me to have an interest in x without it being the case that I have any rights about x. Equally, I have rights that don't seem to relate to any strong interests. As well as Raz, advocates of an interest theory of rights include **Jeremy Bentham** and John L. Austin.

See **Hohfeld, Werner; rights**
Further reading: Raz 1986; Waldron (ed.) 1985

intergenerational justice: The question of intergenerational justice is taxing political philosophers increasingly. It seems clear that our actions have long-lasting effects upon our environment, which are likely to worsen the situation in which future generations find themselves. What sort of **obligations** can we have to future generations?

Obligations seem to arise from our interactions with other people – so that, for example, if Eddie borrows some money from Joe and promises to pay him back, then Eddie is thereby under an obligation to pay Joe back.

If this is the model of 'coming under an obligation' then it might seem reasonable to say that we only have obligations to people who do or say things to us.

But it is common now to hear something different from politicians and especially environmentalists who resist, for example, policies that adversely affect the biosphere in the long term, because of the possible effect on future generations. Depletion of fossil fuels, damage to the ozone layer, and other environmental harms impact much more on future generations than they do on us. The Kyoto Accord is one example of international agreements intended to honour our obligations towards future generations.

It might be possible to avoid the particular issue of distant generations here by recourse to some empirical predictions. It might be said that we ought to preserve fossil fuels just for the sake of our immediate children – or for the sake of reducing congestion now. Then, we would not need to cite the interests of distant generations in support of environmental protection. So we could favour restrictions on the use of fossil fuels just for the sake of our children. But if this is the case, why isn't our moral concern equally applicable to our children's children and, by induction, to all following generations. The point can also be put negatively. If we have weaker moral commitments to those in the remote future, why do those commitments strengthen as the future is less remote?

If obligations only arise from things people do or say to us, then we have no obligations to future generations, since future generations cannot do or say anything to us. So if we have obligations to future generations, it can't be true that obligations only arise from things people do and say to us.

Further reading: Barry 1995; Parfit 1982

J

justice: The question 'What is justice?' – which opens Plato's *Republic* – is one of the constitutive questions of political philosophy. For many, following **Rawls**, justice is the first virtue of social institutions.

For **Aristotle** in the *Politics*, justice counts as treating equals equally and unequals unequally. Justice, on this line, is to do with non-arbitrary, consistent treatment according to the morally relevant properties of the case in question. This directs attention to disagreements about what the morally relevant properties are: are **needs** or **desert** the morally relevant property in determining the distribution of scarce medical resources? Perhaps the morally relevant property will vary according to what it is that we are distributing – as **Walzer** argues. And, while there is much more work to be done, Aristotle's idea is a very good start, and provides a way of understanding of what unjust **discrimination** might entail.

Aristotle's division into corrective justice, rectificatory justice and **distributive justice** is useful, though does not divide the subject up into equally important parts: the primary concern in contemporary politics has been with the last of these. However, there has been some criticism of this focus – **Iris Young** has criticised the dominance of the 'distributive paradigm' in considerations of justice and injustice, and argued for greater consideration to be given not to inequalities of income and resources but to oppression, status and questions of humiliation and shaming.

See **Aristotle; circumstances of justice; desert; discrimination; distributive justice; intergenerational justice; Locke, John; Marx, Karl; needs; Nozick, Robert; Rawls, John; Walzer, Michael**

Further reading: Barry 1995; Rawls 1971

Kant, Immanuel (1724–1804): A German philosopher of the Enlightenment, whose moral theory provides the foundation for much contemporary liberal philosophical thought. Kant's central contribution to political philosophy is in his articulation of a deontological moral theory (see **deontology**) and a kind of contractualism (see **categorical imperative**) which forms the basis of much contemporary liberal thinking about politics. Substantially, Kant was an opponent of despotism, a theorist of cosmopolitan justice and an innovator in theorising relations between states.

According to Kant, the attitude of enlightened despotism might be appropriate to immature children who lack the capacity to know what is in their interests, but it is not appropriate for adults who can determine how they themselves can be happy. This despotism denies the active nature of human beings and their capacity to make and to act on their own judgements about how their lives should be. This capacity ought only to be constrained by the granting of **rights** to others to do the same within a general principle. For example, if my happiness is only secured by lopping off the heads of my fellow citizens, this activity will fall outside the framework of a workable general law – I couldn't grant the same head-lopping rights to others.

According to Kant, equality before the law is compatible with inequality in other areas of life, such as in property. His argument for this is that the law 'is the pronouncement of the general will' so it can only be 'single in form' and it concerns 'the form of right and not the material or object in relation to which I possess rights' (Kant [1793] 1991). The form of right can outline what rules apply to individuals, but it cannot refer to particular individuals, with particular property holdings. If we were to take inequalities of property into account, we would have to introduce *particular* accounts of property holdings into the law, and so it would fail to be *general*.

Kant argues in *Perpetual Peace* (1795) for a universal kingdom of ends – beyond the capacity of any nation state, which would require a sort of cosmopolitan world government and the withering away of the nation state. This internationalism is one of the most attractive features of his political views.

See **categorical imperative; cosmopolitanism; deontology**

Further reading: Flikschuh 2000; O'Neill 1990

Kymlicka, Will: Canadian philosopher known for his attempts to incorporate multicultural concerns into liberal political philosophy. His overall driving concern is with the importance of cultural resources for enabling autonomy. Liberals, says Kymlicka, 'should care about the viability of societal cultures because they contribute to people's autonomy and because people are deeply connected to their own culture' (Kymlicka 1995: 94).

There are two things to notice about this: first, that Kymlicka justifies concern for cultural viability in terms of a separate value, so the justification is an instrumental justification. Second, the value that plays this justificatory role is a liberal one, autonomy. Kymlicka is explicit about this: 'what matters, from a liberal point of view, is that people have access to a societal culture which provides them with meaningful options encompassing the whole range of human activities' (ibid.: 102).

This suggests that the viability of cultures is a concern for liberals only insofar as they are vehicles for the promotion of autonomy – perhaps a one-dimensional view of the concern for cultural viability. Further, the justification for fostering cultural viability offered by the theorist seems out of line with the justification offered by the member of the cultural group itself: it is unlikely that a member of the cultural group would argue that the existence and viability of *her* culture was important 'in order to enhance my set of options and my resources for autonomy'. Rather, the value of the culture for her would come from its specificity (that it is *her* culture) and this seems to be intrinsic rather than instrumental. On one reading, the liberal theorist appears to be checking off societal cultures against a list, passing or failing them on their contribution to autonomy, and allocating political resources on this basis. As a result, it seems that Kymlicka's justification of policies for cultural viability involves 'one thought too many' – just as Williams argues of the utilitarian justification of avoidance of punishment of the innocent (Smart and Williams 1973).

See **multiculturalism**
Further reading: Kymlicka 1995

levelling-down: The levelling-down objection is directed at one sort of policy proposal designed to secure equality. Objectors tend to argue that if the aim is equality, then it is fine to level up, by enhancing the position of the least well off, but it makes no sense to level down: the least well off do not gain, and those who are better off lose out for no reason. The levelling-down objection seems to suggest that some ways of securing equality are both wasteful – because the surplus must be disposed of – and spiteful, driven by envy – since the least well off make no material gain. In this respect it has some affinities with the

harm principle and the Lockean proviso on original appropriation: it seems that no one gains from opposition to these normative positions, and that is why they are rationally held normative positions. It is because of the levelling-down objection that **John Rawls** permits inequalities to exist under the **difference principle**, so long as their existence benefits the least well off.

But there is something to be said, nevertheless, to rebut the levelling-down objection. First, there are often processes which feedback harmfully from supposedly justified inequalities to those who are worst off. Secondly, the supposed benefits of inequalities to the worst off can be slippery. But at a normative level, the objection discounts equality as a value of independent moral worth, attempting to cash it out into utility gains. This runs counter to the concern of some egalitarians who favour equality not because it can be cashed out in this way, but simply because it represents an underlying moral truth – the moral equality of persons.

See **equality**

Further reading: Swift 2001; Temkin 1993; Temkin 2002

lexical priority: Lexical priority (or lexicographical priority) is a term found in **Rawls**'s *Theory of Justice*, and used in discussion of Rawls's theory and liberal egalitarianism. It refers to priority rules like those found in a dictionary. All the words beginning with A precede all those beginning with B. Then, words are ordered according to their second letter. So ordering according to the first letter of a word takes place before ordering according to the second letter of a word. In a similar way, Rawls's first principle of justice, which concerns equal rights to basic liberties, is lexically prior to the second principle of justice, which concerns distribution of social and economic goods. The first principle of justice specifies a distribution of rights, which sets constraints on the distribution of social and economic inequalities: the first principle is lexically prior to the second. The point of these priority relations is to prevent trade-offs between rights and just distribution patterns.

An account of **justice** which involves a plurality of principles with priority relations between them can be contrasted with a conception of justice based on a single principle, such as classical **utilitarianism**.

See **difference principle; distributive justice; justice; Mill, John Stuart; original position; Rawls, John**

Further reading: Rawls 1971

liberalism: A family of ideas which have come to be closely related, though there are varieties of liberalism, some of which are antagonistic to each other. It is perhaps such an unstable notion that it ought to be seen as an essentially contested concept along the lines that W. B. Gallie suggests.

Foundational to liberalism is the idea of individual liberty, which is sometimes problematically characterised as 'negative liberty' though liberals certainly view **autonomy** as a central value. Liberals tend to accept some argument for the legitimacy of state institutions and for an obligation to obey them – differentiating themselves from anarchists. However, they often argue for a separate sphere of human rights, which may not be violated by a government regardless of its level of popular support for doing so – differentiating themselves from absolutists and authoritarians. Liberals favour state neutrality between different comprehensive conceptions of the good, and tend to assert the priority of the right over the good (though there are perfectionist liberals), in particular asserting the importance of the public/private distinction. Liberalism is also marked by a toleration of difference, and by concern for freedom of thought, freedom of expression and equality before the law.

Liberalism fits well with democracy, because of its voluntaristic account of political power, though it is compatible with a variety of forms of democracy.

Historically liberalism has several roots – the account of limited government in **Locke**, **Kant**'s account of respect for persons, and **J. S. Mill**'s attempt to reconcile **utilitarianism** with **democracy** and a private sphere. Today, because it generally opposes a comprehensive theory of the good, liberalism tends to be secular.

It is also important to note a contrast between classical liberalism – the liberalism, for example, of Locke – and modern liberalism as represented by John Stuart Mill, L. T. Hobhouse, T. H. Green, which is much more interventionist and redistributive. Here the antagonisms within liberalism surface: some see welfarism as unjustly interfering with individual liberty, others maintain that a proper concern for substantial liberty on the part of individuals necessitates welfarist interventions.

Communitarian critics of liberalism urge that we take seriously the way that individuals are embedded into social contexts in a way that (arguably) liberals cannot do. Marxist critics suggest that liberalism rests on an implausibly shallow theory of human nature which assumes the permanent existence of the circumstances of justice, when, rather, the task is to abolish them.

See **absolutism; anarchism; authority/authoritarianism; democracy; Kant, Immanuel; Locke, John; Mill, John Stuart; rights; utilitarianism; voluntarism**

Further reading: Waldron 1987

libertarianism: A position in political philosophy which foregrounds individual liberty as the sovereign virtue of a political system. Libertarianism comes in left- and right-wing variants, but both tend to insist on self-ownership, and on some sort of **voluntarism** in accounts of political obligation. Right-libertarianism, which is more familiar and more politically influential is marked by strong hostility towards the welfare state, towards redistribution and towards what is seen as unwarranted state interference into the private lives of citizens. Its proponents are generally relaxed about inequalities of income and wealth, resulting as they do from the impersonal workings of the market. For some libertarians, taxation is often seen, not merely polemically but actually, as theft.

Again, two variants can be distinguished within this variety of political thought – economic libertarianism and social libertarianism. Economic libertarians oppose taxation and state legislation in the market place: they will tend to be sceptical about the claim that background inequalities vitiate supposedly free exchange. Social libertarians oppose the imposition of moral codes onto private activities – they tend to oppose restrictions on drugs, pornography and firearms – and this can lead to some tensions with those who are otherwise their allies on the political right. Amongst the right libertarians – though with qualifications – are found **Robert Nozick** and Jan Narveson. Politically, libertarians sometimes cite the influence of Ayn Rand, the Russian émigré novelist. Left-libertarians also advocate self-ownership, but they seek to reconcile it with some sort of welfare equality, and they do not necessarily oppose state intervention and resource redistribution. The reconciliation between self-ownership and redistribution can be achieved by employing the **control/income rights** distinction, or by adjusting access to holdings so that self-ownership ensures equal outcomes, or by some egalitarian distribution of resources in the first place.

Libertarians direct sharp questions at the liberal-egalitarian mainstream in political philosophy, and have some real-world political influence.

See **control/income rights; Nozick, Robert; rights; self-ownership**

Further reading: Nozick 1974

Locke, John (1632–1704): English philosopher, teacher and quiet rebel. Locke's key works in political philosophy are the two *Treatises of Civil Government* – particularly the second – and the *Letter on Toleration*.

These texts are an indispensable part of the basis of **liberalism**. In the Second Treatise, Locke presents an argument based on a social contract and natural rights, which prescribes limited government, the separation of powers and a right to rebel on the part of the governed. Locke's work also contains important defences of the right to private property and a voluntaristic account of the duty to obey the state which incorporates the idea that we express our consent tacitly. According to Locke, ultimate authority rests with individuals, and is transferred in a contract to the community, which then lends it, on trust, and under certain conditions, to the government. This process secures legitimacy, but only of a limited sort, hemmed in by the conditions of the loan, and by the **natural rights** of the individuals in the first place. Locke's account thus provides a response to both absolutists and anarchists, and is the starting point of much liberal thinking on the state.

His *Letter on Toleration* is one of the best arguments for religious toleration, making general arguments about the freedom of worship and more philosophical ones about the possibility of changing an individual's beliefs through persecution.

Locke was, in addition, a philosopher who had much to say about language, belief, knowledge and metaphysics though his immense contribution – particularly in the *Essay concerning Human Understanding* – does not always cohere easily with his political works.

He has been the target of criticism from both the left and the right. C. B. Macpherson saw him as the ideologist of market individualism, though at the time, with the redating of the *Second Treatise* (see **contextualism**) he was a radical figure. Others on the right have redrawn Locke's account of private property and made him a much stronger advocate of libertarian conceptions of property than seems plausible.

See **authority/authoritarianism; Hobbes, Thomas; liberalism; property; rights; voluntarism**

Further reading: Simmons 1994; Tully 1993

luck egalitarianism: Luck egalitarianism is a position in **distributive justice** associated with figures like Dworkin and Cohen, according to which the proper aim of distributive justice is to equalise outcomes with respect to luck – so that a person who is struck by lightning receives healthcare and compensation – but not with respect to the choices of social agents – so that a person who chooses to surf rather than work ought not to receive compensation for that choice. Luck egalitarians commonly distinguish between **brute luck** and **option luck**, and they need to rely on the ability to distinguish between choice and chance.

Further reading: Cohen, G. A. 2000; Dworkin 1981a; Dworkin 1981b

M

Machiavelli, Niccolo (1469–1527): A diplomat and historian, in service to a series of Florentine rulers. His best-known work is *The Prince*, which falls under a general genre of 'mirror to princes', or guide books on statecraft. It is an indirect response to Cicero's *De Officiis*, and criticises the idea that it is appropriate for the prince simply to practise the Christian virtues. Rather, because of his responsibilities in a world of conflict, antagonism and duplicity, the prince ought to be prepared to be ruthless and to dissimulate. Machiavelli argues that the virtuous prince is very different from the virtuous commoner, and needs to avoid squeamishness when situations require that he acts in a way contrary to ordinary morality.

It is possible to see a consequentialist approach to Machiavelli's claims in *The Prince*, and it is plausibly viewed as a contribution to the debate on **dirty hands**, and on the needs of powerful men, for example, in times of war, to make difficult decisions that will inevitably lead to some deaths, in violation of normal deontological constraints. Whether *The Prince* also validates other less justified actions is open to question.

Apart from *The Prince*, which says little about forms of government, Machiavelli is becoming increasingly well known as a republican thinker: his *Discourses on the First Ten Books of Titus Livius* show him as a prominent and perhaps surprising supporter of republican modes of government – that in order to protect our 'negative' liberty, citizens must become strong participants in the decision-making process, determining their lives through republican engagement. In this respect Machiavelli has been taken up by Quentin Skinner and others as a representative of a way of thinking that is an important foil to contemporary rights-centred liberalism.

See **civic republicanism; consequentialism**

Further reading: Skinner 2001

Macintyre, Alasdair (1929–): Moral and political philosopher whose most important work is the so-called 'virtue trilogy' – *After Virtue; Whose Justice, Which Rationality?;* and *Three Rival Versions of Moral Enquiry.* Of these, *After Virtue* is the most celebrated.

There, Macintyre develops a critique of modernity that centres on the absence of the idea of man as having a proper end or *telos*. This teleological conception is, however, necessary for morality to have a point – without a conception of mankind as having a proper end, morality reduces to a set of rules to enable people to satisfy their preferences.

In order to revive the construction of a conception of man's proper end, and of the virtues, Macintyre argues, at the end of *After Virtue*, for a concentration on small-scale communities committed to common projects.

Liberalism is subject to a penetrating critique in *After Virtue*: **Rawls** and **Nozick** are accused of constructing principles of **justice** without any sense of social embodiment. For them: 'It is as though we had been shipwrecked on an uninhabited island with a group of other individuals each of whom is a stranger to me and all the others. What have to be worked out are rules which will safeguard each one of us maximally in such a situation' (Macintyre 1981: 250).

For these reasons, Macintyre is often seen, with Charles Taylor, Michael Sandel and **Michael Walzer** as a communitarian thinker, though he rejects the label.

The Aristotelian tradition which Macintyre seeks to revive is, in some ways, a conservative one, and Macintyre is open to the criticism that he restricts the scope for external criticism of the moral traditions that he examines. But he rejects this criticism, suggesting that 'reason can only move towards being genuinely universal and impersonal insofar as it is neither neutral nor disinterested, that membership in a particular community, one from which fundamental dissent has to be excluded, is a condition for genuinely rational enquiry, and more especially for moral and theological enquiry' (Macintyre 1990: 59–60).

Macintyre's work has been deeply significant for modern philosophy, linking criticism of the Enlightenment project with **communitarianism** and the revival of **virtue ethics**. It is not necessary to endorse either his Thomism or his positive proposals in order to be challenged by his work.

See **Aristotle; communitarianism; Thomas Aquinas; virtue ethics**

Further reading: Horton and Mendus 1994; Macintyre 1981; Macintyre 1988; Macintyre 1990

Marx, Karl (1818–83): Philosopher and social theorist, who gave his name to one of the most important political movements and analytical perspectives of the last two hundred years. Marx's works cover economic theory and analysis, historical analysis, philosophy and moral theory, political interventions and polemics. Over the span of his writing different phases can be made out. The early works, which were only widely available from the 1950s, such as the *Economic and Philosophical Manuscripts* of 1844, show a mainly humanist ethical and philosophical concentration of ideas. They particularly foreground the notion of **alienation**. The later works, such as *Capital*, consist of detailed economic analysis, aiming to expose the 'laws of motion' of **capitalism**. The intent, though, was political – to encourage and support revolutionary change. A third set of writings – such as the *Communist Manifesto* and the *18th Brumaire of Louis Napoleon*, were designed to intervene in these struggles, and to comment on them. The *Manifesto* was written in collaboration with Frederick Engels, Marx's long-term sponsor and co-thinker.

Marx's aim was to understand capitalism, better to supersede it, and he drew on **Hegel's** and, before him, **Aristotle's** work, in order to understand the nature of that supercession. However, Marx's dialectical approach was couched not at the level of abstract thought but in more concrete and economic terms. As such it has become the touchstone for approaches that start from an examination of the economic and class factors in explaining social change, across sociological theory, philosophy, aesthetics, media studies, amongst other fields.

Politically, the movement to which Marx gave his name went through several mutations, and it is not straightforward to argue that Marx would have endorsed the centrally controlled states of the communist world up to 1989. Despite that, the failure of those states does in some ways reflect on Marx's work if only to make it certain that we can no longer read Marx through the eyes of his immediate contemporary readers and opponents.

See **alienation; false consciousness; Frankfurt School; historical materialism**

Further reading: Cohen 1978; Elster 1985

Marxism: Ideology that takes its roots from **Karl Marx**, though he famously declared that he was not a Marxist. Marxism incorporates both a political movement centred on the working class that strives for an end to class oppression and injustice, an explanatory perspective on the social world, and a normative position which opposes alienation and supports radical social change based on a perfectionist account of man as a sociable and cooperative being.

The political movement has been the most successful and the least convincing of these aspects. From the revolutions of 1848 through to the Paris commune and October Revolution of 1917, along with many further upheavals, primarily in the Third World, revolutionaries have cited a Marxist world-view as the justification of their actions. Successful revolutions led by Marxists have restricted private property, but have often been accompanied by illiberal and undemocratic measures in which human rights have been severely violated. They have, in general, failed to create dynamic productive enterprises, and fallen short on the ideal of emancipating people from alienation in order that they live lives of self-realisation. Dissident Marxists, from Trotskyists to the New Left, to the Frankfurt school have recognised many of these failings.

The Marxist approach to social scientific investigation has been more successful, and is fully incorporated into most social-scientific disciplines.

Within analytical political philosophy, Marxism has been less successful until recently, when **analytical Marxism** has become – perhaps briefly – a respectable school of thought. But ironically, this has taken place at a time when the movement that calls itself Marxist has been subject to huge defeats at the hands of the people it was supposed to emancipate, and this has meant that those who draw on some of Marx's insights are now more likely to characterise themselves as some sort of liberal-egalitarian.

See **analytical Marxism; Cohen, Gerald A.; equality**

Further reading: Cohen, G. A. 1978; Elster 1984; Kolakowski 2005

methodological individualism: A position in the philosophy of the social sciences which has to be carefully distinguished from various sorts of ethical or moral individualism. Methodological individualists hold that the best explanations of social events, processes and institutions are couched in terms of individuals, their attitudes, beliefs and other properties, rather than at the level of groups, classes or institutions. Explanations couched in over-general terms either make illicit reference to social wholes – which are nothing more than aggregates of their members – or are just sloppy shorthand, in the absence of a properly causal micro-level story.

Methodological individualists therefore tend to be very critical of **Marx**'s explanatory method and other sorts of functionalist sociology: **functionalism** seems generally to break with the canons of good explanation prescribed by methodological individualism since functions are possessed within systems, and individualism prescribes the breaking down of systems into their component parts. Methodological individualists are critical of Marx's historical materialism in so far as it seems to rely on functional explanations.

Historically, methodological individualism has been seen to be a good fit with the anti-Marxist, anti-holist right (and it works this way with Karl Popper): however, if it is simply a neutral methodological principle for social investigation, there is no need for it to come with normative baggage, and, recently, theorists influenced by **analytical Marxism** have argued that good explanation must be methodologically individualist in form.

Further reading: Elster 1985; Ruben 1985

Mill, John Stuart (1806–73): An English philosopher and politician, probably the most important historical thinker in the Anglo-Saxon liberal tradition.

Mill's contribution to political philosophy is immense, ranging from the key text about political freedom *On Liberty*, to a fully articulated overall moral theory in *Utilitarianism*, through a trenchant development of democratic *Theory in Considerations on Representative Government*, to pioneering texts of **feminism** – *The Subjection of Women*.

In *On Liberty*, Mill seeks to assert one 'very simple principle' that government interference into the life of the individual ought only to take place when his action may cause harm to others. The individual, on this line, is master of himself and may choose to go to his own hell in any way he chooses. This principle seems to enshrine the liberal concern with individual freedom, limited government and human rights, quite clearly. However, there are problems both with a precise articulation of Mill's central idea – what are these exclusively self-regarding actions? – and also with the consistency between this idea and Mill's **utilitarianism**. It is certainly possible in principle for the **harm principle** to conflict with utilitarian claims, and it seems likely that it would in practice.

Similarly, Mill's defence of representative government and democratic decision making is not as clear as it seems at first sight. He certainly favours an extension of the franchise, but not only does he endorse plural voting for graduates, also he sees democratic institutions as only suitable for a mature polity, exempting 'barbarians' from the advantages of **democracy**. And there is a tension here too, for democracy is defended in terms of its advantages, not on a rights basis, or by reference to deontological concerns with autonomy for its own sake. For a utilitarian, endorsement of particular institutions will always be contingent.

In *The Subjection of Women*, written with his wife, Harriet Taylor, Mill the former radical MP, makes perhaps his most radical contribution to his contemporary political scene. Inveighing against the Victorian restrictions on women's lives, he argues for legal equality and women's suffrage. In this, as in his overall philosophical legacy, he is still an extraordinarily rich and relevant resource.

See **consequentialism; harm principle; liberalism; toleration; utilitarianism**

Further reading: Gray 1983; Ryan 1990

multiculturalism: Multiculturalism commonly refers to two distinct things: first the fact of multiculturalism – the fact that increasingly nation states include those from many different cultures, sometimes geographically concentrated, but sometimes not, sometimes sharing a language with the indigenous population but sometimes not, with all sorts of culturally specific practices, including social linguistic, dietary, educational legal and financial practices.

The second phenomenon that goes under the name of multiculturalism is the advocacy of policies of group rights, or differential treatment, or specific laws that are expected to address the fact of multiculturalism in a positive way. This multicultural politics might be concerned with establishing a framework of exemptions from the otherwise generally binding laws, or it might involve a retreat of the state from areas of judgement which are culturally sensitive, or funding for cultural groups which are under threat. The question arises whether such practices are consistent with 'difference-blind liberalism'. Certainly, there seems to be a tension, though some multiculturalists (for example, **Kymlicka**) argue that group rights are essential for the full participation of individuals in their culture, and that this full participation is necessary if individuals from minority communities are to have the resources available to them to live a full and autonomous life. Others, such as Brian Barry, see multiculturalist policies as anti-liberal and to be condemned on that basis.

Current concerns about free speech, in particular the freedom to publish words and pictures that are offensive to religious minorities, seem to point to a tension between **liberalism** and at least some forms of multiculturalism, since sensitivity to cultural concerns might prescribe restrictions on the practices that liberalism looks to defend. Further, against a background of irreconcilable cultural and religious differences which in some cases is expressed violently, there seems restricted scope for optimism about multicultural prospects for conviviality.

See **autonomy; equality**

Further reading: Barry 2001; Kymlicka 1995; Young 1990

nationality: The property of being part of a nation – a set of people who identify themselves in the same way and occupy territory, perhaps sharing a language and history. The particular necessary and sufficient conditions for nationhood are controversial. Nationality is an issue in political philosophy partly because of the tension between nationalism and a cosmopolitan viewpoint. That tension draws on a more general contrast between impartialism and agent-relative moralities – a problem for all sorts of collective identities, insofar as they are thought to give rise to special obligations and rights. If we are to take an impartial point of view, then judgements about **justice** ought to have universal applicability. Questions of specific national identity ought not, then, to affect those judgements. However, theorists of nationality like David Miller, Roger Scruton and **Alasdair Macintyre** reject this account of the irrelevance of nationality to judgements about justice. They distinguish nationality from various vicious nationalist movements – for Scruton, vicious nationalism is a pathology rather than the normal representation of national sentiment. They argue that a ground-level national affiliation is a legitimate – and perhaps indispensable – part of a coherent structure of **rights** and obligations.

See **cosmopolitanism; multiculturalism; Rawls, John**
Further reading: Caney 2006; Macintyre 1984; Miller, D. 1995

natural law/positive law: Natural law – if it exists – is the law that comes from natural justice, which is independent of, and trumps, the positive law made by men in political institutions. In Roman law, natural law is derived from the *jus gentium* – the law that was thought to apply to all peoples within the Roman Empire, regardless of local customs. It was derived from the writing of the ancient Greeks. For contract theorists, such as **Locke**, natural law is the moral law that governs the **state of nature**. In Locke's view, it is discoverable by human reason. Positive law, in contrast, is the law created by actual legislatures. For Locke, natural law trumps positive law when the two conflict. Some versions of natural law regard it as the manifestation of God's will for us – the line taken, for example, by some Catholic philosophers after **Thomas Aquinas. Kant,** in contrast, aims to deduce natural law from the fact of human rationality, and argues that God must also conform to the objective requirements of a rational morality.

Advocacy of natural law always faces accusations that its source is mystical and arbitrary, yet the claim that individuals have universal natural rights, just because they are human, is widespread and powerful.

See **Aristotle; Locke, John; rights; Thomas Aquinas**
Further reading: Finnis 1980

natural lottery: Term used by **Rawls** and others to illustrate the capricious nature of the distribution of advantages.

It seems uncontroversial to say that we are responsible – and may reasonably be blamed – for what we choose to do, and not for what happens by chance. It seems uncontroversial, too, to say that we deserve to be rewarded for what is the product of our own efforts and not for what happens by chance. Rawls argues that the gifts we receive from the natural lottery – accidents of birth and of genetics – are 'arbitrary from a moral point of view' and therefore that they ought to have no influence on a just distributive pattern. This applies not only to those features of our lives that appear unproblematically to be gifts of the natural lottery – like musical talents but also to some that are more controversial, such as the capacity and ability to work very hard: not everyone has that capacity: those who do are lucky, and have the capacity through no merit of their own: the capacity itself, then, ought not to be rewarded, and the lack of a capacity – congenital laziness – ought not to be a disadvantage in the distribution of scarce resources.

The overall thrust of the idea of a natural lottery has been most clearly appropriated by luck egalitarians who aim to equalise the effects of luck whilst leaving open and uncompensated – unequalised – those differences that flow from the decisions made by individuals. But here the picture starts to get complicated (see **brute luck/option luck**).

See **Cohen, Gerald A.; discrimination; equality; justice**
Further reading: Rawls 1971

natural rights/conventional rights: Natural rights are the set of rights possessed by individuals in the **state of nature**. Conventional rights are rights that are established by social conventions. An example of such a convention is the practice of bagsying whereby rights over the use of, say, a chair, are established by the first person to say 'bags I have that chair'.

See **natural law/positive law**
Further reading: Finnis 1980

needs: To be distinguished from wants, desires, preferences, in that the term 'needs' aims at a much more objective conception of the relation between a subject and an object: I can need something without realising that I need it. Whilst this is important, needs are also always relative to some end: I need X in order to do, or be Y, so that without X, I cannot do or be Y. It is obviously true that I need food and water in order to stay alive, and there are a limited number of basic needs – needs for simple existence – that are objectively specifiable.

But two thought experiments show why this is too minimal a conception of needs: suppose a person is stuck in a small, dark pit, with no escape, and provision of basic nutritional requirements from mushrooms and dripping water. Second, suppose a person is constantly being chased by a man-eating tiger, which he can (successfully and continually) evade only by constant movement. In both these cases very basic nutritional needs are met, but it would perhaps be a mistake to regard these lives as fully human.

But, there are difficulties in the other direction. I may have expensive tastes, so that it may be objectively true that I can't be happy without a ready supply of vintage champagne. In that case, I need Bollinger for happiness, though not for mere existence.

Those who take a capabilities approach to **distributive justice** or who share an Aristotelian or essentialist account of what it is to be human are more likely to have the resources to construct a needs-based account of distributive justice than those whose welfarism is couched in terms of preferences. But distribution according to need, along the lines articulated by **Marx** in the *Critique of the Gotha Programme*, looks more justifiable in some spheres of justice (such as health care) than others (such as holidays). Even where it does apply, it does not touch on the principle of production, and the two principles tend to intertwine.

See **capabilities approach**

Further reading: Hamilton 2003; Wiggins 1987

non-combatant immunity: This is the idea, in the discussion of just war theory, that civilians or non-combatants ought to be considered out of the reach of the contending armies. The principle of non-combatant immunity states that it is never permissible to aim to kill (or severely harm) non-combatants. The principle forbids terrorist as well as counter-terrorist activity aimed at killing (or severely harming) non-combatants. Clearly enough, the principle applies not just to marginal non-state groups but also to states themselves – it suggests a notion of 'state terrorism'. The idea of non-combatant immunity can rest on respect for persons – the idea that only those who have chosen to participate in warfare ought to be targets. Because they have so chosen, combatants are morally culpable. However, there are two problems with this: first, when conscription or measures close to conscription are in place, it is not clear how voluntary the choices made by army recruits are. Secondly, on a strong account of complicity, some tend to argue for much wider culpability beyond those who wear military uniforms. Others argue that the principle of non-combatant immunity is not strong enough. Because it forbids only intentional harming of non-combatants, it remains silent on the foreseen but unintended killing of non-combatants. But this position – that non-combatant casualties constitute unintended and regrettable 'collateral damage' is the standard rationale given by those who justify such acts.

Finally, the principle of non-combatant immunity could be driven by a simple pragmatic concern to minimise harm. Having rules of war will tend to do this, and limiting the reach of intentional killing by widespread acceptance of an exclusion clause will generally minimise harm. But this is a contingent matter, and leaves us with a principle of non-combatant immunity that lacks force in tough cases. Generally, those with strong consequentialist concerns are likely to minimise the force of the principle of non-combatant immunity, and deontological concerns will tend to act in the opposite direction.

Further reading: Walzer 1977

normative/descriptive: An account is normative if it prescribes conduct – if it tells us what we ought to do by laying down norms or criteria by which to judge actions, institutions and so on. An account is descriptive if it simply describes an action, process or series of events. Most philosophers agree, following **Hume**, that descriptive accounts do not entail normative conclusions: how things are does not determine how they should be. But some more recent approaches question this stark contrast: critical theorists argue that the claim to 'value freedom' in the social sciences is a sham, and it is better to be upfront about one's inescapably value-laden approach. In moral theory, virtue theorists take certain general features of humankind to play an important part in determining what virtuous action is, and, in political philosophy, the capabilities approach also reflects on supposed facts about human functionings in determining criteria for global **distributive justice**.

See **capabilities approach; Hume, David; virtue ethics**
Further reading: Rawls 1971

Nozick, Robert (1938–2002): US political philosopher and theorist of distributive justice. Nozick's work covers both political philosophy and other areas – the theory of knowledge, probability theory, and the philosophy of science more generally, but he will be best known for his 1974 publication *Anarchy, State, and Utopia*. In this work he aims to draw the reader in from commonly accepted premises to some surprising conclusions about the impermissibility of redistributive taxation – which amounts to a form of slavery, a minimal conception of the 'night watchman' state, with no welfare component at all, and a strong conception of private property rights which inevitably involves assenting to very wide disparities of wealth, income and resources.

Anarchy, State, and Utopia is a direct response to **Rawls**'s *Theory of Justice* and shares some common philosophical roots – opposition to **utilitarianism** and some affinities to **Kant** and **Locke**. But Nozick's use of **state of nature** theory comes up with radically different results. Individuals have rights, and these ought not to be violated by the state. Redistributive taxation violates these rights – while voluntary redistribution in the form of charity might be commendable, forced redistribution through taxation violates our self-ownership rights. We are entitled, Nozick thinks, to the full fruits of our labours, with only small deductions directed to the state as a protective agency being justified. Otherwise, we are free to pursue our own projects, in voluntary associations, as much as we like. This is justified by a hypothetical but temporal conception of the development of the minimal state. But those associations ought not to coerce patterns of distribution – this would violate the separateness of persons – a violation which, Nozick thinks, is a hallmark of theories like those of both Rawls and the Utilitarians.

Whilst Rawls perhaps won the debate over **distributive justice** amongst academic philosophers, there is little doubt that Nozick won the battle to be politically influential, at least to begin with – his ideas were partially adopted by the so-called New Right in the US and Western Europe in the 1980s and have been influential ever since. Recently there has been something of a revival in interst in Rawls amongst policy makers.

See **Chamberlain, Wilt; entitlement theory; eye lottery; libertarianism**

Further reading: Nozick 1974; Wolff 1991

Oakeshott, Michael (1902–92): The most important English conservative philosopher, Michael Oakeshott is known for his works *Rationalism and Politics* (1958) and *Human Conduct* (1976). Oakeshott aims to pursue a view of civil association which respects tradition and eschews empiricism. He condemns rationalism and ideological attempts to remodel political institutions according to some overarching and historically abstracted universal principle, and argues instead for an approach in which the guiding principles of political associations are discovered rather than made. For example, representative government is not to be thought of as a particular instrument for fulfilling a certain function, to be assessed according to how well it does in relation to that pre-existing function. Rather, it is a form of civil association that is irreducible – itself setting up the nature of the function, and the problem to be addressed. In this (rather Wittgensteinian) way, with civil association not conceived of as the product of contract or of the coordination of individual purposes, but as something more self-generating, the problem of political obligation changes shape. If civil association is the taken-for-granted form of life, political obligation has this character too. Oakeshott's theory of human nature can be elusive, and his criticisms of the left are partly self-standing. He did not present a new system but rather a series of influential insights into the nature of political thinking.

Further reading: Franco 2004; Grant 1990

obligations: Any account of the relations between the individual and other individuals, and the state, or sub-state corporate bodies, will need to give an account to what obligations we are under and how they arise. One standard way to do this is by suggesting that obligations arise from contracts: if I promise to pay you back that money I borrowed from you last night, then I am under an obligation to you to do just that. To the extent that we make promises or quasi-promises to each other and to the state, then we are, to that degree, under obligations. For some philosophers that is the end of the matter: for others, there are also natural obligations, which exist without any prior contract. Amongst these might be duties to one's children – who are not competent to make contracts, and obligations to animals who are in our care and likewise incompetent. It is, though, a little mysterious as to how these natural duties arise: unless they arise from some sort of tacit adoption of a contract, they seem to violate **Hume**'s insistence that you cannot derive an 'ought' from an 'is'.

Obligations fall under the realm of right, as opposed to those actions and institutions of value that are good, but not obligatory: this distinction takes the form in **Kant** of the distinction between broad obligations – to kindliness, for example, which can be met in a variety of ways. Kant contrasts these with strict obligations, which are categorical in form.

To the extent that obligations do not exhaust the terrain of morally commendable actions, there is a contrast between the right and the good: both the idea of a right to do wrong and of supererogatory actions support this way of thinking. One seems to be a case of wrong actions that are morally permissible, the other, of good actions that are not required. If this is the case, we have a two-level moral theory, and there is a need to determine the priority relations between the two levels. **Liberalism** seems to involve this contrast: the sphere of liberal rights protects our right to do wrong, and the liberal insistence on the priority of the right over the good prescribes some limits on state action to secure the good society – our collective obligations, perhaps, do not extend that far.

See **categorical imperative; priority of the right over the good**

Further reading: Horton 1992; Klosko 1994

option luck see **brute luck/option luck**

original position: For **Rawls** the original position is a way of modelling the demands of **justice**. Owing something to the social contract tradition of **Hobbes**, **Locke** and **Rousseau**, it is a hypothetical device which seeks to isolate those criteria which are relevant to an account of just principles from those considerations which are not. The hypothetical participants in the deliberations in the original position know some things, but they are ignorant of others: they are ignorant, for example, of their own sex, race, religious identity (or lack of it) and – most controversially – they are ignorant of their own particular comprehensive theory of the good. They make their decisions about principles of **distributive justice** from behind a 'veil of ignorance'. They do have access to certain empirical features of the world – they have a general understanding of some of the causal social chains that determine the outcome of one policy compared to another. Rawls specifies things in this way in order to deliver an impartial, but achievable, conception of justice, rooted in the real world, but insensitive to those matters that ought not to skew distribution.

The original position has been criticised for its artificiality, its arbitrariness, the fact that it includes too much, or that it excludes too much. Some criticism seems to miss the target – that the original position constitutes a hypothetical decision procedure. Like the agreement 'you cut, I'll choose' when dividing up a cake, it seeks to inoculate the distributor from partiality in advance. Whether that sort of decision properly models the concerns of justice is a moot point. For example, it is arguable that the model of the rational chooser, dispossessed of any notion of the good, is itself a conception of the good – that the sort of life we ought to lead, what the best sort of life is, is that of the rational chooser without a comprehensive conception of the good. But whether the orginal position is 'artificial' is beside the point.

See **social contract**

Further reading: Daniels 1975; Rawls 1971

ownership see **property**

P

Paine, Thomas (1737–1809): Born in Norfolk, and for the first thirty-seven years of his life an unknown artisan, Thomas Paine became a leading figure in the American rebellion against Britain, and also played a role in the French Revolution. Following his desperate emigration to America in 1774, he established a reputation as a pamphleteer and journalist, who was unambiguously on the side of the people. His writing style, no doubt because of his humble origins, was direct and accessible – although he was something of a misfit amongst the gentry-led rebellion, he was also the key populariser of the rebellion. Paine's rationalism and democratic drive led him to popularise the views of **John Locke** and the earlier Commonwealthmen. God had created us with natural rights, distributed equally. High or lowly birth was an irrelevance from this point of view: differences in outcome were justified only on the basis of variations in talent and individual choices. Men of equal status ought to have an equal voice in decisions: social life and cooperation is a natural outcome not an artificial construction – and whilst the state was required when things went awry, its scope ought to be strictly limited.

Returning to Europe, in the late 1780s, Paine's opposition to hereditary power became most widely known with the publication of *The Rights of Man* in 1791. This amounted to a ferocious attack on **Burke** and a defence of the ideals of the French Revolution. For Paine, tradition and custom provided no justification for the thwarting of the will of the people. Republicanism, on the French stamp, represented the future. Not surprisingly, this was a dangerous position to take, and Paine fled England for France.

There, he took the side of the Girondins, but found himself vulnerable and imprisoned when the Terror began. He was released in 1794, and published the *Age of Reason* (1794) which outlined and justified his Enlightenment Deism, before returning to America, and widespread condemnation.

Further reading: Keane 1995

pareto optimality: Pareto optimality describes a criterion for judging distributive arrangements. An arrangement is Pareto-optimal if nobody could be made better off without someone being made worse off. It is named after the Italian economist Vilfredo Pareto. If a situation is Pareto-optimal this shows that there are no pain-free gains available. Pareto optimality rules out, for example, immediate gains from unused resources. If the situation is Pareto-optimal, gains for some must come from losses for others.

However, in any situation of interesting complexity the set of Pareto-optimal outcomes is very large. The condition of Pareto optimality does not help in distinguishing within that set. Thus, even for those who value the criterion, it can only be a necessary and not a sufficient criterion of social justice. Some critics also argue that Pareto optimality takes too much as given, since the criterion refers to outcomes, not processes.

One important result in social choice theory, due to Sen, is called 'the impossibility of a Paretian liberal'. This shows that there is a conflict between the sovereignty of individuals protecting their own private sphere and a weak Paretian condition of efficient allocation.

Further reading: Sen 1970

paternalism: An approach to regulation, law and rights that is modelled on the relationship between parents (perhaps, but unimportantly, fathers) and their children. Parents seem to have natural duties towards their children, are responsible for their well-being, know better than their children how to secure that well-being, and consequently have authority over them. On this line of argument parenting is like a benevolent dictatorship. Paternalism is the thesis that people should be made to live in the way that is best for them – whether they recognise that this is best for them or not.

Legislation that is modelled on this sort of arrangement includes proscription of some drug use, censorship of political material or pornography, and laws that require the use of seat-belts in cars. In each case, it may seem that

Mill's anti-paternalist **harm principle** is violated, and citizens are treated not as rational beings whose autonomy ought to be respected, but as child-like. For this reason, paternalism seems to confront autonomy and respect for rights, the Kantian rationality constraint on our dealings with persons of equal moral value, and the priority of the right over the good.

Paternalist measures can be more easily justified by a consequentialist than a Kantian – but the base line justification is likely to be partly empirical – and sometimes smacks of circularity: paternalism is only justified when people are not capable of rational and autonomous actions (as children are not capable). They need, therefore, to be protected from the damaging consequences of their dangerous actions. The evidence that they are not capable of rational and autonomous action is that they choose to partake in the hazardous activities in the first place.

In 'Two Concepts of Liberty' (1969), **Berlin** tries to show how a certain way of thinking about liberty has, paradoxically, led some political theorists to adopt paternalism. Berlin believes that this way of thinking is dangerous, but Taylor defends it.

See **autonomy; positive liberty**

Further reading: Berlin1969; Taylor 1995b

patriarchy: Literally rule by the fathers – patriarchy is a term used largely but not exclusively by second-wave feminists to describe a systematic structure of rule by men. This is manifested overtly: most powerful positions in society are held by men, most decisions are taken by men, politics is a male preserve, aspects of family and divorce law posit men as more powerful – but patriarchy manifests itself less obviously in a set of discourses, narratives, stereotypes and underlying assumptions – from the seemingly trivial use of terms like 'chairman', applied both to men and women, to the widespread social acceptance of forms of mutilation like surgical breast augmentation and female genital mutilation.

See **authority/authoritarianism; feminism**

Further reading: Okin 1991; Pateman 1988

perfectionism: The view that certain states or activities of human beings such as knowledge, achievement and artistic creation are good, apart from any happiness they bring and that what is morally right is what best promotes these excellences or perfections. In political philosophy, a perfectionist view might lead to advocacy of state support of high culture – such as state funding of opera – since such subsidy supports the best form of life.

Within political philosophy, it is common to come across a version of this doctrine (such as, in different ways, in **Marx** and **Aristotle**) founded on a conception of essential human nature. Once we know what essential human nature is like (perhaps that we are essentially aesthetic, or contemplative, or productive beings) then we can set up political institutions and rules to support the flourishing of those activities. Perfectionism tends to lead to both self- and other-regarding duties. These other-regarding duties will be duties to promote perfections and they seem to conflict with liberty and equality. A generalised version of perfectionism might incorporate a conception of positive freedom that licences infringements of autonomy in order to secure the good for others, despite their own wishes.

But this is not necessarily the case. A perfectionist account could involve **autonomy** centrally in its conception of the good life. Thus, a perfectionist could give an account of rules and principles of justice that aims to encourage autonomy, which could, in practice, map out the same territory as an anti-perfectionst, pluralist account.

See **pluralism; priority of the right over the good**

Further reading: Raz 1986

Plamenatz, John (1912–75): Plamenatz would have characterised himself as a social and political theorist, rather than as a political philosopher. His strength lay in the exposition, elucidation and criticism of the canonical works of the Western tradition in political thought – **Machiavelli, Hobbes, Locke, Rousseau,** the English Utilitarians, **Hegel, Marx** and Weber. The output of work in this area accounted to the largest contribution to the subject by anyone in Britain since the Second World War. Whilst he rejected linguistic analysis, Plamenatz's approach was more robust about testing for validity and truth than the contextual school, who argued that ideas cannot be correctly interpreted without the fullest possible understanding of the motives, intentions and circumstances of those who express them. Plamenatz held that, while this contextual information might be of some help, it was not essential to the interpretative task.

Consent, Freedom and Political Obligation (1968) examined the role of consent in securing obligation. In this work, Plamenatz tied the notion of consent closely to the idea of giving permissions and expressing wishes. Later, Plamenatz took this analysis to be too narrow, and he attempted to explain the case in which someone who voted for an election candidate who turned out to lose could be taken to have consented to rule by the winner. Clearly the voter did not necessarily express any wish concerning the winner. Nonetheless, Plamenatz held, he had in some sense consented to the authority of the winner.

In *Man and Society* (1963), Plamenatz argued that **Locke** had brought together two functions of consent that ought to be kept apart. It was right to stipulate consent as a condition for bringing individuals within the bounds of society but false to claim that, in a constituted society, an obligation to obey rested on having consented to obey. In *The English Utilitarians* (1949), Plamenatz is critical of **Mill**'s claim to rest his anti-paternalistic principles on a utilitarian basis. Such principles simply do not provide a secure basis for anti-paternalism, because the choice for or against anti-paternalist principles is a contingent one.

Further reading: Plamenatz 1968

Plato (c. 428–348 BC): Ancient Greek philosopher, arguably the founder of political philosophy. In the *Republic* argues against democracy and for Philosopher Kings as the basis of an ideal state. In the *Laws*, he gives a typology of constitutions illustrated by the various Greek city states.

The *Republic* starts by inquiring into the nature of **justice**. For Plato, justice is not the same as power, and it provides a standard by which power can be judged. In this respect Plato sets up a mode of criticism that has been directed against absolutists and autocrats for millennia. However, Plato is no democrat, and is scathing about the Athenian constitution.

Plato characterises **democracy** as like democratic man – rather chaotic, and inconstant – though his liberty and equality are commended. This is a move used throughout the *Republic*, where Plato compares the sort of man characteristic of certain political frameworks: democratic man, aristocratic man and so on. But there is also a clear argument by analogy – the practice of governing a state is like the practice of navigating a ship. Both require particular sorts of expertise, training, experience and knowledge, which are not generally possessed. Because of the particular sorts of skills required, it would be very foolish to entrust a ship to a quarrelsome crew, who lacked those skills. In the same way it is imprudent to entrust a state to its people. They lack the expertise, training, experience and knowledge to guide a state, and so will make a worse job of it than an elite of philosopher-kings who are properly equipped for the task. In short, the common people are not up to the job of guiding the state in the most effective way.

Plato presents a typology of constitutions – timocracy, based on honour, oligarchy, based on wealth, and democracy based on licence – but all fail in comparison with the rule of philosopher-kings. This constitution rests on a highly developed educational system which prepares the citizen for the task of ruling.

In arguing for his ideal state, Plato proposes the abolition of the family, and some form of communism, as well as censorship and what we would today call propaganda on behalf of the state. The organically conceived state penetrates into every part of the citizen's life, in a way that, to some commentators such as Popper, foreshadows totalitarianism.

See **aristocracy; democracy; justice**

Further reading: Annas 1981

pluralism: Pluralism refers to the idea of multiplicity of basic things, in opposition to monism. Moral pluralism refers therefore to a series of basic moral values that are incommensurable – not comparable to each other – and not reducible to each other. The existence of irreducible pluralities of value will mean that political conflicts are likely to be intractable. For example, it is often thought that both freedom and equality are of fundamental value, but that it is not possible to reduce or assimilate one to the other. Thus, and in practice, they conflict, leading to irresolvable political conflict. The view that value pluralism makes conflict inevitable is countered by monistic views that assert the existence of a sovereign virtue, which will, perhaps, be uncovered and understood. If this is the case, perfectionist accounts of the good life may be appropriate.

Pluralism also refers to a distinctive idea in political science – the idea that political power is, or ought to be, distributed amongst a number of different centres or institutions, each acting on the other and restricting its activity. On this account, institutional pluralism is thought to be a bulwark against tyranny.

Further reading: Baghramian and Ingram 2000

political obligation: A political obligation is a moral obligation to obey a state's laws and perhaps also to support the state (by paying taxes and sharing in common defence, for example) irrespective of whether one has independent reasons for doing so. The primary philosophical questions regarding political obligation concern when and why a person might be under such an obligation.

Why should one obey the state? This is perhaps the most fundamental question in political philosophy. There are a number of answers offered, but one way of avoiding the question is to consider areas in which there is independent moral reason for acting as the state requires: it is wrong to lop off the heads of passers by, not merely because it is against the law to do so. One might even worry about someone who only refrained from head lopping because it was against the law to do so. Rather than this sort of case, political obligation tends to consider whether there are any independent reasons for obeying the law, regardless of the content of the law itself. These reasons are likely to be procedural – the law is likely to be authoritative because of how it has come into being. So, perhaps the law comes from God, or God's representative – by **divine right** – on earth, and that gives us a reason to obey it. Or perhaps we are the authors of the law ourselves, by consenting to or participating in the process by which the law is made: on this line of argument we are ruling ourselves, and so the question of political obligation appears to pose a contradiction – why should I obey a law that I prescribe? However, voluntarist theories of this sort tend to lose the individual will somewhere in the complexities of the contracting or consenting process. Forms of consent that clearly deliver the goods – like express consent – are difficult to generalise. Plenty of people do not expressly consent to obey the law. Those forms of consent that are easily generalisable – **tacit consent** – seem not always to deliver the obligation goods.

Some consequentialists believe they have an adequate theory of political obligation, because they point to the devastating effects of lawlessness in human happiness and welfare. But not all acts of lawlessness are problematic in this way if there are victimless crimes. Consequentialists need to deduce objections to individual law-breaking from the consequences of general law-breaking, and it is not clear that they have the resources to do so.

H. L. A. Hart's **fairness principle** seems to go someway to formalising some of our intuitions about political obligation: the state, after all, is a joint enterprise from which we all reap benefits – even presumptive benefits.

But perhaps the most interesting work on political obligation suggests that we adopt a plural account, with a series of different perspectives brought to bear on different aspects of the problem, and different specific obligations to obey. But there are two criticisms of this approach. First, it seems unreasonably *ad hoc*. Secondly, the perspectives are in tension with one another.

Philosophical anarchists are able to side step this difficulty entirely. In practice, they may end up obeying the law in almost all cases, but they will not do so simply because it *is* the law.

Further reading: Hart 1955; Horton 1992; Wolff 1970

positive law see **natural law/positive law**

positive liberty: Conception of liberty standardly – but sometimes misleadingly – contrasted with negative liberty. Following **Berlin**'s famous essay 'Two Concepts' it is common to contrast two conceptions of liberty – negative liberty, thought of as 'liberty from', and positive liberty, commonly thought of as 'liberty to'. However, following MacCallum's criticism, this seems analytically inadequate. Positive liberty covers at least two conceptually separate ideas – one is freedom as **autonomy** – my ability to rule myself – and the other is having the resources that will enable me to take up the opportunities that are available.

In the history of political thought, positive freedom has been subject, as **Berlin** rightly suggests, to exploitation by totalitarians. In the form of freedom as autonomy, it is possible to see an attempt for a higher self to control a lower self – if I am subject to cravings, or base instincts, which I would like to control but am unable to do so, then perhaps I am not fully free. The totalitarian turn comes where the higher self is not internal to the individual itself, but becomes embodied in the person of the state. Then, because of this 'monstrous impersonation' the state stands in as the higher self and directs the actions of the lower self – the individual citizen in the name of the latter's positive freedom. Thus positive freedom can seem to be implicated in coercion – the suggestion that one is 'forced to be free' in **Rousseau**'s words.

Despite this, there is something in different varieties of positive freedom – it is commonly invoked by republican figures as an argument for political participation as a prerequisite of freedom and autonomy.

See **Berlin, Isaiah; civic republicanism; negative liberty**

Further reading: Berlin 1969; MacCallum 1967; Taylor 1995a

postmodernism: The name given to a wide-ranging and diffuse way of thinking that covers aesthetics and architecture, music and politics, literary theory and the analysis of moral thinking. In political philosophy, postmodernism can best be summarised as 'incredulity towards meta-narratives' in the words of Jean-François Lyotard. The grand narratives to which postmodernists express incredulity include, *inter alia*, **Marxism**, Freudianism, Scientism, the Enlightenment project, the quest for single, universal criteria of rationality and for abstract and general principles of **justice**. Behind each of these grand narratives there is the suggestion of dominating and essentialist discourses which aim at subordinating other ways of looking and thinking. They rest on the ideas that texts have preset meanings, that words have essential referents and that capturing the authors' intentions gives us a way of accessing the truth. *Au contraire*, Wittgenstein has shown that meaning is use, Barthes has proclaimed the death of the author and Adorno and Horkheimer have implicated scientific rationality in the worst evils of our times.

Postmodernism is post *modern* because these grand narratives are associated with modernity and the aspiration to rational, universal thinking, well founded in essential facts about the human condition. But if there are no essential facts – if essentialism is another dominating and exclusive discourse, if anti-foundationalism is the best response to the plurality of normative thinking, then the whole theoretical project of modernity looks inadequate.

Amongst the important postmodern thinkers are Foucault and Derrida, Julia Kristeva, Luce Irigary and Jean Baudrillard. The impact of postmodernism on political philosophy is impossible to determine impartially. In one respect it has left the discipline entirely alone – Anglophone political philosophy of the type practised by **Rawls** is itself a 'grand narrative', to which postmodernists simply express incredulity. These expressions are often greeted with incomprehension by Anglophone political philosophers.

At the same time critical theory and critical theorists have engaged with mainstream political philosophy in an exciting and unproblematic way. To the extent that postmodernism is reflected back into political philosophy through **Iris Marion Young** and **Jürgen Habermas**, it has a profound effect on Anglophone political philosophy. To the extent that it is represented by the sorts of thinking exposed by the Sokal affair, in which the editors of *Social Text* were happy to publish a nonsensical paper, the interaction will be minimal.

See **Foucault, Michel; foundationalism; Habermas, Jürgen; Young, Iris Marion**

Further reading: Boghossian 2006; Drolet 2003

power: Power is exercised when one social actor is able to get another social actor to conform to his wishes. In an influential account, Steven Lukes outlines three dimensions of power, according to which, first, power is recognisable when there is social conflict, second, power can be exercised when conflict is suppressed, and, third, power can be recognised when an individual's real interests are damaged, even if the person consents to or approves of that damage. On this account, power is a paradigm of

W. B. Gallie's essentially contested concept, because the notion at its heart – of an individual's real interest – is essentially contested. It is plausible to suggest that simple lack of knowledge of counterfactuals and also ideological illusions can cloud individuals' understandings of their own real interests. Workers may be victims of false consciousness, women may internalise the assumptions and stereotypes of **patriarchy** and adaptive preferences can obscure the exercise of power.

Critical theorists, drawing on **Foucault**'s analysis, have drawn attention to these and other ways in which power is exerted, directing attention away from simple force and coercion to the more subtle and sophisticated ways in which power is (perhaps unwittingly) exercised by dominant groups. But insofar far as these accounts rest on controversial and contested assumptions about real interests, they will remain contentious themselves.

See **coercion**

Further reading: Lukes 2004

primary goods: Primary goods are those goods that everyone wants, whatever else it is that they want. So for those behind the **veil of ignorance**, in the **original position**, the distribution of primary goods can be assessed without knowing about their own comprehensive theory of the good. Amongst those on **Rawls**'s list of the primary goods are basic rights and liberties, freedom of movement and occupation, powers and prerogatives of office, income and wealth and the social bases of self-respect.

For some critics, listing primary goods in this way seems a little *ad hoc* – resting on an illegitimate essentialist account of human nature that smuggles in too much empirical information. For others, such as Sen the list is too short and lacks sufficient detail – it is possible to say much more about capacities for functionings that are required to secure human well-being in a wide variety of circumstances.

See **capabilities approach**

Further reading: Rawls 1971; Sen 1995

priority of the right over the good: On the liberal conception of **justice**, a distinction can be made between, on the one hand, different conceptions of the *good* life for human beings – what is virtuous or of benefit to human beings – and, on the other hand, principles of justice concerning what is *right*, what rights and obligations individuals have to one another. Further, it is generally part of the liberal conception that the right is prior to the good – that we ought first to secure individual's rights, and only then promote whatever it is that constitutes the good life. In **Rawls**'s *Theory of Justice*, this is embodied in the lexical priority given to fair **equality of opportunity** over the **difference principle**. More thin conceptions of **liberalism**, such as that articulated in Rawls's *Political Liberalism* have very little to say about comprehensive conceptions of the good, whilst some thicker conceptions, such as those of perfectionist liberals like Jo Raz, argue for a comprehensive conception that involves the thought that the autonomous life is the good life. In this way they bring the two conceptions of moral value closer together.

The priority of the right over the good issues in the simple thought that, whatever the benefits and however much government action might promote the good, there are limits, prescribed by justice, on the extent to which individuals can be incorporated for that end. It therefore expresses a core idea of liberalism and reflects the fact of a plurality of comprehensive conceptions of the good.

See **justice; liberalism; perfectionism**

Further reading: Rawls 1971; Raz 1986; Sandel 1985

prisoner's dilemma: The name given to a core example in **game theory**. Suppose two individuals engage jointly in committing some crime: both are caught, but, with no evidence, the police must seek a confession from one of the prisoners in order to prosecute the crime. The prisoners are held separately without the means of communication, and each is offered a heavily reduced punishment if they are the first to confess. Each therefore reasons as follows: if I keep quiet and he confesses, I face a heavy sentence; whereas if we both keep quiet, we will both be freed. But if he might confess, then I ought to confess first, in order that I, and not he, receive the reduced sentence: he might confess, so I should make sure I confess now.

For the two prisoners acting in consort, the best option is for neither of them to confess. But for each of them individually, the best option is indeed to confess, and as fast as possible. Where there is a gain from breaking an agreement, individuals acting alone and thinking of their own short-term interests are likely to break that agreement. Prudence in these circumstances tends to undermine cooperation – cooperation requires the establishment of moral norms – such as the doctrine of honour amongst thieves.

The prisoner's dilemma is one way (albeit anachronistically) of modelling the situation in the **state of nature**, according to **Hobbes**. Influential accounts have used game theory as a way of justifying political authority.

Further reading: Hampton 1986

property: Property rights are the strongest rights that an individual can have over a thing (or, in the case of slavery, another person). These rights are an aggregate of several distinct sets of claim rights, correlative duties, privileges and immunities (see **Hohfeld**). But the main ones are the rights to use and to exclude others from use, the rights to exchange or give away, and the right to destroy.

Questions arise about the forms of property – common ownership, private property, non-ownership, and the justification of these forms. As well, questions can be asked about the distribution of property rights, questions which fall under the general concern with **distributive justice**, and over the original process of appropriation – or making something into a piece of private property. Here **Locke** sets the standard, arguing in the second treatise that individuals can make something into property if they mix their labour with it, so long as two conditions are met: first, that the appropriation leaves others with 'enough and as good' left over for further appropriation and, second, that what is appropriated is not wasted. If these two conditions are met, it looks as if original appropriation can take place without harm to anyone's interest, and so it might seem unreasonable to oppose it. There is a real question, though, about the extent to which the two provisos – particularly the first – can be satisfied. Depending on how it is interpreted, Locke's claim can underwrite forms of communism, or give support to widespread private property and the inequalities that go with it.

Conflict over private property goes back as far as **Aristotle** and **Plato**'s disagreement over common ownership, and features among the concerns of all the canonical figures. For **Rousseau** and **Marx**, private property is to be condemned – it alienates social individuals from each other, and has subtle detrimental psychological effects. For **Hayek**, private property is the foundation of a free society.

See **alienation**

Further reading: Becker 1977

prudence: The idea of an act being prudential is often contrasted with the idea of an act being moral. For example, it is prudent not to eat rotten food, but not eating rotten food seems neither to be a moral obligation nor particularly morally praiseworthy. Prudence is the virtue of the rational egoist who aims to maximise his own satisfaction. In political philosophy, some contractarian accounts of political and moral obligation seem to establish a prudential rather than a moral obligation, and this means that the basis of the obligation is less secure. Prudential justifications of acts will depend on the consequences to agents: prudential justifications of the obligation not to steal will work only as far as the state apprehends thieves and punishes them. On this line of argument, prudence is also the virtue of the clever knave, who acts in accordance with principles of **justice** only insofar as they match his own satisfaction, and breaks them when he can get away with it.

See **assurance game; contract theory; Hobbes, Thomas; prisoner's dilemma; state of nature**

Further reading: Gauthier 1986

public/private distinction: Distinguishing between the public and the private realm is a mark of most kinds of liberal approaches to the problems of political morality. One way of making the distinction is to outline the extent to which we are publicly accountable for our actions, and consequently governed by principles of **justice** that govern the 'basic structure', and to contrast those realms in which we are not so answerable. In this respect, private life is protected by individual rights. Critics charge that this leaves huge areas of injustice and oppression hidden from scrutiny, whilst defenders of the distinction suggest that extending the scope of justice endorses an unreasonable **paternalism**.

For **Marx** in 'On the Jewish Question' (Marx 1944), the split between the state and civil society leaves liberal man with a split personality, alienated from his essence as a social and communicative being. Theorists of multiculturalism add complexity to this picture: group rights accorded to cultural minorities may provide resources that allow individuals to live autonomous lives, but run the risk that they thereby permit unjust practices in the private sphere. Some liberals worry about this, and join feminists and Marxists in arguing that the 'personal is political'.

In determining the boundaries of the private sphere we also help to determine the areas in which partiality is justified. We may reasonably prefer our children to others in some matters: by reading them, and only them, bed time stories. We may not reasonably prefer them by appointing them to well-paid government jobs, when we have the power to do so. The extent of this legitimate partiality is contentious, partly because it sets in train an inegalitarian dynamic that leads to unequal opportunities.

See **equality of opportunity; Marx, Karl**
Further reading: Barry 2001; Okin 1991

punishment: Punishment requires moral justification, since it involves the infliction of hard treatment (pain, financial loss, the removal of specific freedoms) on an individual against their will. There is, then, a problem of justifying punishment as an institution, which underlies the particular problem of what punishment is appropriate in individual cases. There are three standard theories: deterrence, rehabilitation and retributivism. Deterrence theories are found in the works of consequentialists such as **Bentham** and retributive theories are found in **Kant**, amongst others. The recent history of the problem shows a move in philosophy and penal theory from deterrence and rehabilitation to the 'new retributivism'.

One of the reasons for this is that deterrence theories seemed unduly influenced by the light-mindedness with respect to **justice** evidenced by utilitarian accounts of punishment. On these accounts, justice seems to be only a contingently derived outcome of a system of punishment. Further, deterrence theories seemed to violate the rationality constraint, which, drawing on some Kantian considerations, prescribes that rational persons be treated as ends, not merely as means. Rehabilitation and reform accounts of punishment also seem to fail in this way, however, if they bypass treating the individual as a rational person. This has given rise to theories of punishment as communication, in which great emphasis is place on the role of the person being punished, and their coming to a full understanding of the ways in which they have violated important moral constraints. An institution of punishment created in this way would treat offenders as rational persons, not as reactive animals who required training and modifying in order to secure preferred forms of behaviour.

See **consequentialism; deontology; justice; Kant, Immanuel; utilitarianism**

Further reading: Matravers (ed.) 1999

R

race: While racial categories and ethnic identities are part of our everyday discourse, it is hard to say what a 'race' actually is. Genetic difference does not map to racial categories – there is no 'racial gene' that allows us to read off racial categories.

However, race is obviously a major source of self- and other-identification and a way in which the world is carved up, conceptually, socially and economically. Races are groupings of human beings into categories according to morphology and genetics. Groups are characterised as 'white', 'black' and so on, on the basis of skin colour and facial features.

Race is largely a social construction, which selects certain characteristics and clusters groups around them. This contingency is one way of understanding – and undermining – the idea of a racial hierarchy. Racial hierarchies mean that advantageous and disadvantageous treatment is distributed depending on membership of a racial group. But, since the characteristics that determine membership of a racial group are clustered together on an arbitrary basis, discrimination on the basis of race is itself arbitrary (and consequently unjust).

However, this is too simple an approach. In fact, what makes racial discrimination especially troubling is the fact that this set of characteristics does constitute and help to determine the individual's life chances across a very wide range of variables: housing, healthcare, education, job opportunities and so on. The more these cleavages coincide on racial grounds, the less satisfactory it is to dismiss racial groups as arbitrary and simply irrelevant from the moral point of view.

In so far as **difference-blind liberalism** fails to take into account the background conditions, structures, hierarchies and patterns of oppression and domination, it will, to that extent, risk reflecting them and leaving them in place. In so far as difference-blind liberalism fails to reflect the idea that individuals are essentially constituted by racial identity, then it fails properly to represent them in its decision procedures. This is the sort of case made by critical race theorists against difference-blind liberalism.

See **discrimination**

Further reading: Appiah 1996; Boxill 2000

Rawls, John (1921–2002): Rawls is the most important political philosopher of the twentieth century. He spent virtually his entire career at Havard, and published a series of works that form the *locus classicus* of contemporary liberal political thought. His most important work is probably still *A Theory of Justice* which reinvigorated political philosophy at the time of its publication in 1971. The theory expounds the basis of a liberal and roughly egalitarian state on the basis of a **contract theory**, reviving the traditions of **Hobbes, Locke, Rousseau** and, most closely, **Kant**. In doing so, Rawls turned the tide of utilitarian thinking in political philosophy. Rawls's model introduces key techniques and methodologies to political philosophy which are outlined elsewhere. His is a contract theory in which individuals behind the **veil of ignorance** choose principles of **justice** and **lexical priority** relations between them. This model is designed to conform to revised intuitions about social justice reached through a process of **reflective equilibrium**. The principles that arise are a commitment to liberal **rights,** to **equality of opportunity** and to the **difference principle**.

In more recent work, Rawls has refined his approach, expressing his commitments a little more cautiously (some say to their detriment). In *Political Liberalism* (1993), he argues that liberal theory ought not to aim at **perfectionism,** but that liberal institutions are justifiable as the outcome of an overlapping consensus amongst individuals who do not share the same comprehensive theory. In *The Law of Peoples* (1999), Rawls extended his concerns from the principles of justice that ought to cover a single state to the concerns about international justice. Communitarians and libertarians provide the most comprehensive critics of Rawls's views, the former condemning the abstraction and atomism that is thought to vitiate his method, the latter condemning his endorsement of redistribution.

See **distributive justice; justice; original position; reflective equilibrium**
Further reading: Daniels 1975; Pogge 2006; Rawls 1971

reflective equilibrium: Method of evaluating and formulating theories of **justice** propounded by **John Rawls**. It seems a mistake to allow pre-theoretical intuitions to determine the success or failure of a theory, for it may be that our intuitions are misplaced or in contradiction with one another. However, it also seems to be a mistake to allow formulations of general rules to trample over intuitions by requiring their constant and wholesale revision. Rawls's suggestion is that we work towards a point where settled intuitions and general principles are in 'reflective equilibrium', each open to revision, but with neither trumping the other.
See **original position; Rawls, John**
Further reading: Rawls 1971

representative democracy: A form of democracy in which representatives of the people make decisions on their behalf. Representative democracies are common ways of constructing legislatures, because of the practical problems of securing direct democratic decision making, but the nature of fair representation is contentious.
Amongst the issues involved in designing a representative democracy are: the method of choosing the representatives; the influence of parties; the frequency of the elections and the relationship between the representatives and (on the one hand) those they represent and (on the other hand) the executive and judicial functions of government. Should representation be 'proportional' rather than skewed by political parties – and, if so, proportional to what? Does it matter if the representatives do not

reflect the electorate in terms of class, sex, ethnicity and so on?

If my representative differs from me on an issue, then I am faced by Wollheim's paradox of **democracy**. In any case, handing over my authority to someone to act in my name seems at least potentially to involve a loss of **autonomy**. Thinking along these lines persuaded **Rousseau** and others since to regard representative democracy as a process in which the people gave up their rightful power to representatives with their own specific interests. On this line of argument, representative democracy seems to involve an **alienation** of political power. One response is to insist on a process of mandation or of delegation with rights to recall, rather than endorsing the much looser tie of representation in which the sole source of accountability is the chance to reject the representative when they come up for re-election.

In contrast, representative democracy sometimes seems to combine the need for democratic accountability to the people with the need for stability in government, and expertise amongst legislators and professionalism within the political class. Government by referendum, on this account, is a recipe for capricious decision making.

See **deliberative democracy; democracy; voluntarism**
Further reading: Held 1996

rights: Key term in liberal thought. Rights conjure up the idea of a protected sphere of activity within which the rights holder may do as she chooses. The core idea of a right is that of an entitlement. If I have a right to X, then I am entitled to X and I ought not to be prevented from doing X. Rights may concern the not-doing of actions, and they may be held by other people.

So if I have a right to smoke, in a certain area (and, perhaps, other things being equal), no-one may interfere with me smoking. If I have private property rights over a toothbrush, no-one may use that toothbrush without my permission.

Controversy surrounds the *grounding* of rights and two theories here confront each other: the will or choice theory and the interest theory. Others regard both theories as false, arguing that rights are not fundamental categories but are provisional and undergirded by consequential or procedural justifications: rights are justified insofar as they are a way of securing good consequences, or rights are constructs of legal procedures, and have no independent moral existence.

See **Hohfeld, Werner; liberalism; natural law/positive law; right of nature; right to do wrong; rights, theories of**
Further reading: Steiner 1994; Waldron (ed.) 1985

rights, theories of: There are two front-running theories of rights: the will theory and the interest theory. Each aims to answer the question, 'What do rights do for those who hold them?' Interest theorists argue that the point of a right is to further the interests of the rights holder. Will theorists argue that rights protect choices.

There are various versions of a rights-founding theory that founds rights in the exercise of will or autonomy. Will theorists assert that a right gives its holder power over another's duty, and that this is its function. Further, they think that rights give the ability to control what others must and must not do. But there are two problems with this approach. If rights are all about the power of the rights holder, then it seems odd for there to be unwaivable rights – rights over which the rights holder specifically lacks power (the power to waive the right). But there seem to be such rights – such as the right not to be enslaved. Though some philosophers differ on this, the thought of an unwaivable right seems to be coherent, in which case rights cannot solely be grounded in the will. A second problem is that the will theory seems to deny rights to non-rational beings, or incompetents, perhaps to infants and animals. This conflicts with our ordinary understanding of at least some rights, such as the right not to be tortured.

See **interest theory of rights; rights**
Further reading: Waldron 1985

right of nature: The Hobbesian natural right, or right of nature, is the absence of any obligation not to do a thing. It is often useful to analyse a particular right into its component parts: a series of moral relationships between the rights bearer, the activity concerned, and other moral actors. One basic relationship is the 'liberty right' to the action itself, and this right is the absence of a duty to refrain from that activity. So it might seem that a liberty right to smoke in a particular area would be indicated by a sign saying, 'Smoking Permitted'. This sign would mean that I did not have a duty to refrain from smoking in that area.

But **Hobbes** means more than this when he outlines the right of nature. For the notice saying, 'Smoking Permitted', also puts a constraint on other people: it means that they must put up with the smokers in that area. Hobbes's right of nature does not include this constraint on the activity of others. If we both had full Hobbesian liberty rights, I would be allowed to smoke and you would be allowed to try to stop me. What would be missing is any moral constraint on you or me, any sense of not being allowed to do certain things. Hobbes's right of nature is like a sign, hanging up in the **state of nature** which says, 'Anything Permitted'.

See **natural rights/conventional rights**
Further reading: Finnis 1980; Hobbes 1996

right to do wrong: Is there a right to do wrong? Do those who picket the funerals of US servicemen, claiming that their deaths are a result of US toleration of homosexuality, act wrongly, but within their rights? If there is, then we seem to be committed to a two-level moral theory, in which autonomy (the right to do wrong) sometimes trumps the judgement of the individual act. The existence of a right to do wrong will be a problem for some unsophisticated consequentialists, such as act-utilitarians.

See **consequentialism**

Further reading: Waldron 1981

Rorty, Richard (1931–): Richard Rorty is one of the most important of US philosophers, out of the leftist tradition and advocates pragmatism in the tradition of Dewey.

Rorty's social thought is in some ways rather conventional American liberalism, in which he celebrates the end of ideology. This fits with his opposition to looking for secure foundations for knowledge – his 'anti-foundationalism', and can be tracked back to his first major work: *The Linguistic Turn* (1992). The argument is further extended in his major work, *Philosophy and the Mirror of Nature*. If philosophy turns linguistic, then this is likely to have dire consequences for political and philosophical views that see philosophy as the mirror of nature, and think that nature provides secure foundations for radical social change. Thus he attacks the whole project of a realist theory of knowledge and the incursion of 'scientism' – a crude natural scientific model of knowledge – into the humanities, including philosophy.

In 'The Priority of Democracy to Philosophy', Rorty defends **Rawls** against the communitarians and, unsurprisingly, attacks perfectionist accounts of the good life.

Rorty is enormously prolific, and is a public intellectual, engaging in political controversy and accessible writing. In *Philosophy and Social Hope*, which is part autobiographical, he writes for a general audience on political and moral matters, articulating a pragmatist and liberal – and distinctively American – account of social life.

Further reading: Calder 2007; Geras 1997; Rorty 1979; Rorty 1989; Rorty 1992

Rousseau, Jean-Jacques (1712–78): In *The Social Contract* of 1762 Rousseau aims to show how men can be free under the rule of law. Like other social contract theorists he contrast the state of man in the **state of nature** with the state of man in a governed society, but the comparison is not to the advantage of the latter. Man, who is born free, but everywhere is in chains, seems to lose freedom with the advent of private property and government, even representative democratic government. This can only be overcome if, somehow, we rule ourselves. The mechanism for this is the general will. If we each think carefully and impartially about the best interests of the society as a whole, then we will come to discover the general will. In acting in accordance with the general will, we act in accordance both with our best interests and in accordance with our own will.

There are two features of Rousseau's society that are essential if his system is to function. First, the citizens of Rousseau's society are equal before the law. Second, they are also roughly equal with respect to their social standing and economic circumstances. It is only if this is the case that the citizens will be truly *independent* of each other. True independence is needed if the citizens are to make laws as their reason dictates. This is because social and economic inequalities allow the wealthy to put pressure on the poor, with the result that neither rich nor poor have the common good in mind when they choose which laws to enact. Here, Rousseau's views contrast with those of the liberal: on liberal views, what matters is equality before the law; equality before the law is compatible with all kinds of social and economic inequalities. Rousseau also delivers a criticism of representative government – those who follow Rousseau often argue for forms of direct and participatory **democracy** in order to narrow the gap between citizens and the decisions that, according to Rousseau, they alone have the right to make.

See **civic republicanism; general will; liberty; social contract; voluntarism**

Further reading: Bertram 2003; Dent 2005

S

self-ownership: Self-ownership refers to the idea that persons own themselves. The principle that persons own themselves is a foundational principle for many libertarians, it is defended by some liberals, and it has great importance for distributive justice. If persons own themselves, it seems reasonable to say that they own their talents and abilities. If they own their talents and abilities it seems to follow, on many accounts of appropriation, that they own the fruits of those talents. But, since there is a wide variety of talents and abilities, then there will be a wide variety of returns to individuals. So the claim that individuals own themselves seems to licence widespread inequality. Moreover, self-ownership seems to fit well with some of our intuitive responses to speculations about the use of body parts (**eye lottery**).

The most important historical discussion of self-ownership is found in **Locke**'s *Second Treatise of Civil Government*, where he asserts that 'every man has a property in his own person'. The idea also seems implicit in some socialist accounts of exploitation, which condemn capitalist theft of what the worker rightly owns – the fruits of their labour. **Robert Nozick** has asserted the thesis that individuals own themselves, and argued that self-ownership is a necessary condition for securing respect for persons. Because this thesis leads to unequal holdings, and because those unequal holdings can justly be transferred by consenting adults, he has endorsed the ensuing unequal distribution of resources as just.

Both the notion of self-ownership and the thesis that we own ourselves have been criticised, however. It is arguable that, although this is my right hand, I don't, in any clear sense, *own* it because ownership mischaracterises the sort of relation I have to it. Further, it is suggested that what is at stake in concerns about the control of my body parts is best characterised as individual autonomy, not the infringement of a set of property relations. Finally, the account of appropriation associated with self-ownership has been criticised.

See **Chamberlain, Wilt; Cohen, Gerald A.; distributive justice; equality; entitlement theory; eye lottery; Locke, John; Nozick, Robert**

Further reading: Cohen 1986; Nozick 1974

social contract: The notion of a 'social contract' – a contract made by citizens to transfer certain rights to a state – provides a way of considering the rights and obligations of a state towards its citizens, and their rights and obligations towards it.

Hobbes's, **Locke**'s and **Rousseau**'s accounts of the social contract can each be divided into two related accounts. First, each provides an account of the *purpose(s)* of the contract. More specifically, each argues that the contract must fulfill a certain purpose, or certain purposes, because life without a state, in a **state of nature**, would be intolerable in certain ways. For example, Hobbes argues that the purpose of the contract is to overcome certain causes of 'war' in a state of nature. Secondly, each philosopher provides an account of the *content* of the contract. This includes claims about (1) *which rights* are transferred by the contract, (2) *to whom* they are transferred, (3) *with whom* the contract is made, and (4) whether the contract is *revocable* and, if so, *when*. For example, Locke claims (1) that the contract transfers the natural right (and duty) to enforce certain moral rights, and (2) that this is transferred to a government.

Contract theories have been widely criticized for the artificiality of the model by which they seek to establish the justification and legitimacy of a state. But the status of this criticism is difficult to pin down. Contract theorists can accept the charge of artificiality, and sensible ones will do so, yet argue that it misses the point of securing rational foundations. More sophisticated critics, including communitarians, will question both the desirability and the sense of playing the hypothetical contract game, when there are other and better resources on which to draw, either in facts about human nature, moral traditions, or elsewhere.

See **consent; fairness, principle of; Hobbes, Thomas; Locke, John; Rousseau, Jean-Jacques; political obligation; state of nature**

Further reading: Boucher 1993; Hampton 1986

socialism: Socialism is a term that now refers to a diffuse family of ideological positions associated with the political left. Amongst the common features of this family of views is: some sort of commitment to common ownership of the means of production, a commitment to equality and, more specifically, often a commitment to some sort of equality of outcome or welfare equality, and political and social collectivism. It is perhaps easier to mark out socialist thought from its critics on either side: unlike communism, socialists do not advocate either the abolition of private property in entirety, nor do they forsee, or intend, the violent overthrow of the capitalist state. At the same time, unlike social democrats and liberal egalitarians, socialists do not concede that the essential levers of economic control would remain in private hands. However, because the term now has considerable ideological weight and emotional appeal, but little or no precise analytical value, it is approaching redundancy in political philosophy.

See **anarchism**

Further reading: Parekh 1975

speciesism: Term coined by Richard D. Ryder which aims to connect human attitudes to animals and plants with forms of unjust discrimination between different individuals within the same species – such as racism and sexism. Thus speciesism as a term seeks to trade on the antipathies towards racism and sexism and harness them to the idea of unjust discrimination against non-human animals. The critique of racism did not deny any differences between races, just as sexism did not deny biological differences between sexes. However, it did deny that such differences were morally relevant, or that they ought to determine distribution of powers, rights resources and so on. Likewise, the term speciesism seeks to deny that the obvious differences between species are relevant to their moral status.

Obviously, the degree to which this charge hits home will depend on the account of moral relevance that is offered. For some utilitarians the question of moral status reduces to the question of the avoidance of pain. Since non-human animals clearly feel pain, then a non-speciesist account of **justice** will give a high priority to their interest in not feeling pain, and so on. But, in contrast, if moral value is said to derive from a rational capacity, such as an ability to formulate moral principles or to use language or some other Kantian formulation, then the dividing line will fall differently. However, it won't fall at the species divide, and this is the point of the charge. On a rational capacities account, both babies and those suffering very great mental impairment will be denied the concern which is properly owed to other humans. Whichever way the moral cut goes, it does not seem to coincide with the species divide. Consequently, species-specific attitudes and forms of behaviour seem just as arbitrary as racism.

See **discrimination; justice**
Further reading: Singer 1995

state of nature: It is not surprising that the state of nature forms a component part of many structured conceptions of political philosophy: essentially it involves understanding what the world would be like in the absence of political authority. There are at least three aspects to this. One sort of state of nature concerns the way in which humans behave before the institution of political authority – in order to discover this, anthropological and archaeological work needs to be done. The second is to consider what happens to societies when political order breaks down: concrete examples of mass looting after natural disasters give support for a pessimistic evaluation here. But lastly, the state of nature refers to a hypothetical condition which is useful for discussing several different questions, including: the purpose of the state, and the needs that must be met by the state that cannot be met in the state of nature; the limits of the state – the justification of infringements of natural autonomy, the role of morality in the shift from the state of nature to a political society, and the mix between those obligations and duties that are natural and those that are the product of social relationships.

Whilst **Hobbes**, **Locke** and **Rousseau** all drew on anthropological and historical data in specifying their pictures of a state of nature, it is the third hypothetical and abstracted conception that does the real work in contemporary political philosophy. Thus both **Rawls** and **Nozick** employ state of nature theorising, but in markedly different ways. For Nozick, the state of nature is a quasi-historical phenomenon, which lays down limits on the possible establishment and development of the state. For Rawls, the closest to a state of nature theory is his conception of the **original position** – where the surrogate state of nature acts as a decision procedure in establishing principles of **justice**.

The power of a state of nature hypothesis stems from the way in which it analytically differentiates between political societies and human nature. But this is precisely its weakness: not only communitarians but also those who seek a more empirically freighted theory will find state of nature theorising excessively abstract.

See **Hobbes, Thomas; Locke, John; Nozick, Robert; original position; Rawls, John; Rousseau, Jean-Jacques**
Further reading: Boucher and Kelly (eds) 1994

state of war: Is the **state of nature** a state of war? **Locke** makes a clear distinction between the state of nature and the state of war and there seems a fairly clear reference to **Hobbes** ('which however some men have confused') in §19 of the Second Treatise. The key difference is this: if individuals in the state of nature behave rationally – that is – according to the law of nature, then it will be a state of peace. But unfortunately they don't. The state of peace falls apart because of irrational action that is contrary to the law of nature. (For **Hobbes** the state of war was not a product of irrational but of rational behaviour.) Irrational people who harm others for their own gain, or fail to get the proportions right when they avail themselves of the executive power of the law of nature, resort to force contrary to the law of nature. And it's the use of force contrary to the law of nature, in the state of nature, that transforms it into the state of war. Nonetheless, for Locke, that use of force, though it might be likely, is not inevitable. However, Locke is perhaps a little ambivalent in his account of the state of war, and it is easy to see why. He is pulled towards giving an optimistic account of life in the state of nature, by the need to defend only limited, not absolute government. But he is pulled to giving a pessimistic account, because if the picture is too rosy then there is no incentive to leave the state of nature. For Locke then, we are faced with a series of inconveniences in the state of nature.

See **Hobbes, Thomas; Locke, John; social contract; voluntarism**

Further reading: Boucher and Kelly (eds) (1994)

sufficiency: In an important article called 'Equality as a Moral Ideal', Harry G. Frankfurt suggests that egalitarians misidentify the morally relevant properties of distributive arrangements. We should not ask whether these arrangements manifest equality, but whether there are *sufficient* resources for individuals. He analyses the notion of sufficiency in some depth, making it clear, for example, that there may be arrangements of holdings where equality acts against the interests of everyone involved, by condemning all to the equality of certain death. Equality is no good to us if we all have insufficient resources for life. Like **Nozick**, Frankfurt directs some of his argument directly against **Rawls,** arguing that 'the only morally compelling reason for trying to make the worse off better off is, in my judgement, that their lives are in some degree bad lives.' But the worse off may not have bad lives. It may be that those who are worse off still have sufficient, in the sense that it may be reasonable for them to be content with having no more than they have. A concern with ensuring that people have sufficient may, therefore, cut against egalitarianism.

See **capabilities approach**
Further reading: Frankfurt 1987

T

tacit consent: Term used by **John Locke** and others to derive a political obligation in the absence of expressly undertaking one. Locke's argument is that when you do a certain thing or series of things you in fact silently consent to have obligations placed upon you. Express consent is given by saying, 'I agree to obey the government.' Tacit consent is given when I do X, and X entails or means or equals saying, 'I agree to obey the government.' In particular, Locke thinks that by quietly enjoying the protection of the state you give it your tacit consent.

Tacit consent is not the same as a derivation of political obligation that looks at first quite similar; the notion that we should obey the government because it is *fair* to do so. See **principle of fairness**. In the case of tacit consent, the putative subject of the government does some act and that act means or entails or equals consent to the government. On the fairness account, something received by the putative subject entails that she owes obedience to the government. There is no intermediate step where doing or receiving something is held to entail consent. So, on the fairness account, one might want to suggest that receipt of state benefits incurred an obligation to obey the government because it would be fair to do so. But one need not say that consent was given at the same time as the benefits were received. On the tacit consent account, a disobedient subject is doing something contradictory whereas on a fairness account a disobedient subject is ungrateful.

Further reading: Simmons 1976

teleology: A theory is a teleology if it posits an entity with a proper or natural purpose (telos) or end. Those theories that understand human society as having a proper end to which we either are or ought to be directing our energies are teleological theories. If the purpose or end is a moral one, then teleological theories provide a reason for adopting perfectionism as state policy: the state ought to do what it can to promote the end state, to get our lives to match up more closely to the end state. Moral teleologies of this form are found in almost all religious conceptions of the good society, in Aristotelian and essentialist accounts, in **Marx**'s account of a society in which distribution is on the basis of need and **alienation** is abolished, and in one variety of perfectionist liberalism in which the good life is identified as the autonomous life. Teleological theories of this form can be contrasted with theories of **justice** that insist on the priority of the right over the good.

Teleological theories also occur in the philosophy of social explanation, where they aim to explain social phenomena in terms of their ends or functions. This is controversial. In some cases, where a conscious social agent, with aims and purposes, lies behind a teleological explanation, that teleological explanation seems solid. In other cases, where the explanation involves the summoning up of a conscious actor, or just the hope that some mechanism might be discovered at a later date, the accounts provided by teleological objections look flawed.

See **functionalism; Macintyre, Alasdair**
Further reading: Macintyre 1981

Thomas Aquinas (1226–74): A medieval theologian and thinker who revived Aristotelian thinking and articulated a political philosophy based on Natural Law.

His most important work is the *Summa Theologiae* a massive account of the theological and philosophical basis of the state – which is formed by four types of laws: eternal law, natural law, divine law and human (positive) law. One crucial contrast in this scheme is between human (positive) law and natural law, which is given by God. If the two conflict, then the positive law cannot be binding, so that any earthly authority must be limited by the constraints of natural law. In this way, and despite his Aristotelianism, Thomas Aquinas prefigures **John Locke** and natural right theorists who formulate a roughly liberal account of limited government.

Thomas Aquinas's most discussed work nowadays is his elaboration of just war theory. Unusually he attempts to apply natural law to the regulation of relations between states, and this leads him to articulate the basis of justified warfare between two enemies. He goes on to make the crucial distinction between the justification of going to war, *jus ad bellum*, and the justice of various actions taken within a context of war, *jus in bello*, in a way that is still of primary concern to theorists – and politicians – today.

See **Aristotle; natural law/positive law**
Further reading: Kenny 1980; Walzer 1977

toleration: The demand for religious toleration is associated with the Enlightenment, and rational, liberal values and principles of **justice**. It is perhaps most strongly articulated in **Locke**'s *A Letter concerning Toleration*, in which he argues that toleration is required not only because suppression of religious disagreement is unjust but also because it is impossible, and the attempt to secure it is counterproductive. However, Locke excludes atheists from toleration, since they are not to be trusted.

Mill presents a less exclusive case in *On Liberty*, where he makes a comprehensive case for freedom of expression, and the toleration of both dissent and of 'experiments in living' – alternative lifestyles, belief structures and so on. The defence offered by Mill is roughly utilitarian in nature: dissent, debate, argument help us to get at the truth of a matter, and for that reason ought not to be repressed. But this is a contingent theory of toleration, according to which a strong case is still possible for suppression of those viewpoints which do turn out to pose as serious danger – perhaps forms of violent religious fundamentalism. Contemporary advocates of toleration more commonly point to value pluralism – the existence of many reasonable and incommensurable moral views and comprehensive doctrines – rather than consequences, as the basis for toleration.

Critics of toleration range from some perfectionists and natural law theorists, to some feminists who argue that some forms of expression undermine other valuable goods. There is, further, a nagging doubt about the possibly patronising connotations of toleration; to urge toleration is to urge that people put up with something that they do not like – that they tolerate a burden, or inconvenience, like a bad smell. But this can be disrespectful to those who are tolerated – it certainly differs from an authentic acceptance or even a welcoming of religious difference as in itself valuable.

See **expressive freedom; harm principle**

Further reading: Horton and Mendus 1991; Waldron 1993

tyranny of the majority: Term found in **Mill** to describe a flaw or drawback to some forms of **democracy** – that if the majority is to decide everything, and the source of legitimacy and moral authority comes solely from the majority, then those who fall in the minority face unfettered and authoritarian power. The problem is particularly acute where there are persistent minorities.

There are ways of understanding the problem that tend to minimise it: for example, there is the optimistic assumption that minorities will not emerge – that those in the minority on one measure will find themselves in the majority on another. But these are not fully convincing, and institutional safeguards and limits are often proposed. The most common is a set of constitutional rights, specifying minimal spheres in which autonomy is protected. So, rights to life, to due process, to free speech and expression, to assembly, to vote and so on are protected prior to the actions of the majority. The actions of the majority are required to respect those rights, and are subject to judicial review in order to ensure that they do so.

Other ways in which the tyranny of the majority can be tempered include **Rousseau**'s insistence that the general will have only general aims – that it not pick out, for example, a particular racial group. For civic republicans, one of the best ways of resisting the tyranny of the majority is to encourage and develop participation in political life – where people are engaged in the political decision-making process they are less likely to be the victims of oppressive decisions.

Finally, there are governmental restrictions on the tyranny of the majority that arise from the separation of powers. Despite all this, there is a need to avoid the sense that the measures put in place are simply *ad hoc* attempts to restrict the popular will, with no basis in **justice**.

The problem of the tyranny of the majority is a serious difficulty for democratic theory – majoritarian democracy can conflict with the core ideas of **liberalism**, with human rights and general principles of **justice**. This is a worrying state of affairs, particularly for those who advocate increasing the scope of democratic decision making. Participative democrats, industrial democrats and direct democrats all need to consider how to respond to the charge that, when they increase the area in which democratic decision making operates, they increase the area for the majority to tyrannise.

See **civic republicanism; democracy; rights**
Further reading: Held 1996

utilitarianism: Doctrine in moral and political philosophy associated with **Jeremy Bentham** and **John Stuart Mill**, and perhaps the most influential philosophical position at affecting public policy. Utilitarians judge the moral value of acts, institutions and/or rules according to their consequences (so utilitarianism is a brand of **consequentialism**) and particularly according to their contribution to general utility. The famous formula that utilitarians seek the greatest happiness of the greatest number is indeterminate, because it invokes two variables – are utilitarians to prefer greater happiness for a smaller number, or lesser happiness distributed amongst more people? It also gives rise to problems of measurement – whilst it may be possible to compare preferences for one individual, who may be able to opt between different bundles of utility-providing resources, or to say that he is indifferent between bundles, the problem of interpersonal comparison remains. Utilitarians are likely to push for objective and measurable criteria that serve as proxies for utility. But this separates out utilitarianism conceived of as a criterion of rightness and utilitarianism conceived of as a decision procedure.

In political philosophy, whilst utilitarianism does seem to point to some rough ways of deciding about public policy issues through cost-benefit analysis, it has a persistent problem in securing reconciliation with our thinking about **justice**. Concerned solely with the consequences of our actions, institutions and rules, utilitarians may be impelled, depending on contingent and empirical considerations, to favour unjust social arrangements, such as punishing the innocent or breaking promises. More sophisticated accounts of utilitarianism, such as rule-utilitarianism, may attempt to swerve around this problem by citing side effects of unjust treatment which mean that such treatment is not conducive to maximum utility. But, even if that is the case, they are open to the charge that they oppose injustice for the wrong reasons – that they have 'one thought too many' as Williams puts it.

The attraction of utilitarianism in public policy arises from its concern with the actual consequences of political action: utilitarians will prefer the outcome that generates maximum utility, even when this conflicts with other valuable ends. But this means that opponents of utilitarianism must favour sacrificing utility – perhaps sacrificing the welfare levels of real people, making them less happy, fulfilling fewer of their preferences, giving them less of what they want, in order to satisfy the demands of some abstract principle such as justice. In this way, opposition to utilitarianism can have a whiff of sanctimoniousness.

See **act utilitarianism; Bentham, Jeremy; consequentialism; Mill, John Stuart**
Further reading: Smart and Williams 1973

Utopia: Utopia is a term originally coined by Sir Thomas More in the book of the same name. A Utopia is a vision, or an account, of a perfect world. Utopian thinking about what the world could, or should, be like, functions in several different ways. First, utopian thought generates aspirations, and consequently acts as a motivation for change. Second, utopian thinking gives an exemplification of an account of human nature: utopian societies are human societies and so reflect what must be trans-historically true about human nature, and not the historically specific features of individual social forms. Third, utopian thinking provides a point of view from which to assess and criticise actually existing societies – by means of constructing a 'critical utopia'. **Rousseau**'s *Social Contract* has been interpreted in this way.

Criticism of utopian thinking centres on the obvious charge that utopianism is unrealistic – prompting the obvious thought that this is precisely what it is supposed to be. What matters is whether the utopian model in mind is possible or impossible, not whether it is realistic or unrealistic. Thus utopianism in political philosophy requires an (Aristotelian) distinction between what is necessary and what is accidental. Critics of particular Utopias will then make the cut between accidental and necessary properties of human societies in different ways. A slightly different tack is taken by Engels in *Socialism: Utopian and Scientific*. There, he is critical of the disconnection in utopian socialist thought between the account of the new society and the agency of change.

Further reading: More 1995

veil of ignorance see **original position**

violation see **infringement/violation distinction**

virtue ethics: Virtue ethics is coming to be recognised as the third big theory, alongside **deontology** and **consequentialism** in the contest between rival moral theories. Its origins lie in both **Aristotle** and **Plato,** and its resurgence is marked by the publication of Elisabeth Anscombe's article on 'Modern Moral Philosophy' in 1958. Its contemporary proponents include, in different ways, Bernard Williams, **Alasdair Macintyre** and Rosalind Hursthouse.

Virtue ethics starts not with acts and their consequences, or with rules and our duties to act in accord with those rules, but with character, and the nature of the virtuous agent. Following Aristotle, theorists tend to examine individual virtues – courage, charity and **justice** and ask how the courageous, charitable or just person would act in such and such circumstances. Because of the concern with the character of the individual moral agent and scepticism about abstract and impersonal rules of justice, it can look as if virtue ethics has little to say about public policy or the just society more generally, and so has little to contribute to political philosophy. But this would be a mistake. Not only have virtue ethical approaches informed the debate about an ethics of care, which is taken seriously by very many theorists of public policy and interpersonal relations (including feminist theorists). But also, if the good society is a society of virtuous agents, then the educative and regulatory structures of our own societies need reform to advance that end.

See **Aristotle; care ethics**
Further reading: Hursthouse 1999

voluntarism: In political philosophy, an account of legitimate
government and our obligation to obey the law which
rests on voluntary action. On a voluntaristic theory,
obligations arise from actions freely taken by those who
become obligated.

In the beginning, political power lies with the individual. It belongs to each individual separately. We own ourselves, and are the masters of ourselves individually and
equal in this respect with others. Political power then can
only be created if we hand it over to someone else. We say
something like 'I give you permission to boss me about.'
In other words, it is absolutely crucial to show that the
institution that makes the laws has our consent. One
aspect that political philosophers often want to emphasise about this account is its *voluntarism*. A theory of
political obligation is a sort of voluntarism if it involves
the voluntary handing over of power from a subject to a
sovereign power.

This all sounds plausible. It suggests an answer to the
question, 'why should I obey the law?' that goes like this:
'You should obey the law because you agreed to. By your
own consent, you handed over the power of governing
yourself to the state.' It is necessary to supplement the
theory with a series of reasons about why I would hand
over this power: for **Locke,** these are reasons to do with
the incommodious quality of the **state of nature**. But the
big emphasis here is on the voluntary nature of political
power. Political power is held by the state, the police and
so on *with my consent*. Because I have consented to them,
I should obey them.

This understanding of voluntarism should not be confused with the use of the term voluntarism, often by

Marxists, to denote and criticise accounts which overplay the importance of the human will and down play, for example, economic constraints. These sort of charges concern the best explanation of events and processes, and are thus descriptive whereas voluntarism in the theory of political obligation has normative content.

See **Locke, John; social contract**

Further reading: Hampton 1986

Walzer, Michael: American political philosopher with interests in the nature of **justice,** international conflict (including just war theory), **democracy** and the foundations of ethical judgements. Walzer argues that **distributive justice** ought to be sensitive to the meanings inscribed in different social goods, and that differences in these meanings may dictate differences in the patterns of justice. But while this may seem to suggest a form of cultural relativism, he also affirms the importance of a minimal code which prohibits cruelty, genocide and slavery regardless of the cultural context. Walzer's key works are *Just and Unjust Wars*, *Spheres of Justice* and *Interpretation and Social Criticism*, and he is an editor of *Dissent* which presents an anti-totalitarian version of radical social democracy.

See **Communitarianism; distributive justice**

Further reading: Walzer 1977; Walzer 1983a

welfarism: View that ascribes to the state some responsibility for securing the well-being or welfare of its citizens. It is of comparatively recent origin, since the prevailing view of liberals up until the nineteenth century was that the state had a rather minimal role in securing general well-being. But liberals such as Hobson and Hobhouse, together with social democrats and socialists such as R. H. Tawney, representing the newly enfranchised working class generated pressure for the extension of the state's responsibilities by the mid twentieth century. In the UK, welfarism has led to the institution of the National Health Service and benefits for those who find themselves unemployed. Politically, welfarism is opposed by those who argue for a minimal or nightwatchman state, those who deny that there are social and economic rights that have a non-contractual origin, and right-libertarians. Others who endorse welfarism and the welfare state see a need for redistribution to combat the effects of the natural lottery and **brute luck**, and argue that only the state can adequately fulfil that role. They deny that they are thereby illicitly endorsing **paternalism,** arguing that contractualist decision procedures would justify quite wide state provision.

In analytical political philosophy, welfarism has a related meaning, referring to those liberals who are commited, in their account of the respect to which moral agents are owed equal treatment, to welfare or well-being as the appropriate measure of that equality.

See **Nozick, Robert**

Further reading: Nozick 1974

Wollstonecraft, Mary (1759–97): English philosopher and feminist: in 1790 Wollstonecraft published a *Vindication of the Rights of Man*, in which she replied to **Burke's** *Reflections on the Recent Revolution in France*. In it she argued for Reason against Prejudice and against privilege and hierarchy, supporting the ideals of liberty and equality which she drew from the French Revolutionaries. She is better known for the publication in 1792 of the *Vindication of the Rights of Woman*, in which she condemned the secondary role forced upon women by men, and the education and behavioural norms laid down by men which kept women in a submissive position. Women – who were rational beings – ought to reject such a role.

Wollstonecraft's work and her reception mark her out as a pioneer of the early feminist movement.

See **Burke, Edmund; feminism**

Further reading: Wollstonecraft [1792] 2004

workmanship model: A model of morality and rights which rests on an analogy between God and human beings to show that property arises from the maker's rights. The supposed fact that we are created by God – and his workmanship – has implications for our moral status. For example, we are prohibited from committing suicide. Equally, the fact that I have worked on a particular piece of wood to make a chair has implications for the moral status of the chair. It is my workmanship, and belongs to me and I may prevent others from using it.

See **Locke, John; property**

Further reading: Simmons 1994; Tully 1993

Y

Young, Iris Marion: Iris Marion Young's seminal and controversial article 'Polity and Group Difference' (Young 1989) is one of the key papers in the emergence of a philosophically grounded critique of **liberalism**. In this paper and in her books such as *Justice and the Politics of Difference* (1990), Young makes the case for 'differentiated citizenship', that is, a conception of citizenship in which rights, for example, for political representation, are not uniform but vary between groups and are distributed on a special, group basis. She asks why, historically, the extension of equal citizenship has not led to social justice and equality. Her prescription of special group rights and a heterogeneous public arises from her diagnosis of this gap between equal citizenship and social justice.

Young's methodology is some distance from the standard Anglo-American analytical approach to philosophy, because she is quite strongly influenced by continental theorists such as **Foucault**. She writes from a perspective more accurately described as critical theory rather than analytical philosophy. One way in which this is manifested in her work is that she often does not start from general principles that would be acceptable to all persons, in a way that **Rawls**, for example, aims to do, at least in *A Theory of Justice*. Young summarises her approach in the introduction to *Justice and the Politics of Difference*: 'Because I understand critical theory as starting from a specific location in a specific society, I can claim in this writing to be neither impartial nor comprehensive. I claim to speak neither for everyone, nor about everything'. Whilst influential both on political theorists and on political philosophers, Young's work was sadly cut short by her early death.

See **Habermas, Jürgen**
Further reading: Young 1990

Z

zero-sum game: A game theoretic concept, in which the outcome of conflict is always zero: if one player wins, others must incur an equivalent loss. In a two-player game, the gain for one player just is the loss of the other player. Zero-sum games are contrasted with positive-sum games – in which either both players gain or the gain from one player outweighs the loss of the other. It is controversial as to whether some conflicts – such as the management/worker conflict – are zero- or positive-sum games. Marxists will tend to argue that they are zero-sum games, but some advocates of industrial democracy will suggest that increased worker participation in decision making, for example, can have positive effects for both players.

Further reading: Hampton 1986

zoocentrism: A view of the objects of moral concern that centres on animals. If we accept the argument presented by those concerned about **speciesism**, then we will wish to consider the moral status of animals. One reason for doing this would be to decide that sentience was a defining moral attribute that made an entity worthy of moral consideration. Moral consideration would then involve regarding animals as of moral worth. Then we will be driven towards a zoocentric ethic. It is worth noting that this does not necessarily involve granting rights to animals – it is, of course, possible to think of animals as worthy of moral consideration without attributing to them properties that might be a necessary condition of having rights.

See **anthropocentrism**

Further reading: Carter 1999

Selected Bibliography

Anderson, Elizabeth S. (1999), 'What Is the Point of Equality?' *Ethics* 109 (2), 287–337.

Annas, Julia (1981), *An Introduction to Plato's Republic*, Oxford: Oxford University Press.

Anscombe, G. E. M. (1958), 'Modern Moral Philosophy', *Philosophy* 33, 1–19.

Appiah, Anthony (1996), *Color Conscious: The Political Morality of Race*, Princeton: Princeton University Press.

Arneson, Richard J. (1989), 'Equality and Equal Opportunity for Welfare', *Philosophical Studies* 56, 77–93.

Baghramian, Maria, and Ingram, Attracta (eds) (2000), *Pluralism*, London: Routledge.

Barry, Brian (1973), 'John Rawls and the Priority of Liberty', *Philosophy and Public Affairs* 2, 274–90.

Barry, Brian (1995), *Justice as Impartiality*, Oxford: Oxford University Press.

Barry, Brian (2001), *Culture and Equality: An Egalitarian Critique of Multiculturalism*, Cambridge: Polity.

Baumeister, Andrea (2000), *Liberalism and the Politics of Difference*, Edinburgh: Edinburgh University Press.

Becker, Lawrence (1977), *Property Rights: Philosophical Foundations*, London: Routledge.

Bentham, Jeremy (1843), 'Anarchical Fallacies', in John Bowring (ed.), *The Works of Jeremy Bentham*, Edinburgh: William Tait.

Bentham, Jeremy (1988), *A Fragment on Government*, ed. J. H. Burns and H. L. A. Hart, introduction by Ross Harrison, Cambridge: Cambridge University Press.

Berlin, Isaiah (1969), 'Two Concepts of Liberty', in *Four Essays on Liberty*, Oxford: Oxford University Press.

Bertram, Chris (2003), *Routledge Philosophy Guidebook to Rousseau and the Social Contract*, London: Routledge.

Bessette, Joseph (1980), 'Deliberative Democracy: The Majority Principle in Republican Government', in Robert A. Goldwin (ed.), *How Democractic Is the Constitution?*, Washington DC: American Enterprise Institute for Public Policy Research, 102–16.

Boghossian, Paul (2006), *Fear of Knowledge: Against Relativism and Constructivism*, Oxford: Clarendon Press.

Boucher, D., and Kelly, Paul (eds) (1994), *The Social Contract from Hobbes to Rawls*, London: Routledge.

Boxill, Bernard R. (1978), 'The Morality of Preferential Hiring', *Philosophy and Public Affairs* 7, 246–68.

Boxill, Bernard R. (2000), *Race and Racism*, Oxford: Oxford University Press.

Burke, Edmund (1985), *Reflections on the Revolution in France: and on the Proceedings in Certain Societies Relative to that Event*, ed. J. G. A. Pocock, Indianapolis: Hackett.

Calder, Gideon (2007), *Rorty's Politics of Redescription*, University of Wales Press.

Caney, Simon (2006), *Justice beyond Borders: A Global Political Theory*, Oxford: Oxford University Press.

Carter, Alan (1999), *A Radical Green Political Theory*, London and New York: Routledge.

Christman, John P. (1994a), 'Distributive Justice and the Complex Structure of Ownership', *Philosophy and Public Affairs* 23, 225–50.

Christman, John (1994b), *The Myth of Property: Toward an Egalitarian Theory of Ownership*, Oxford: Oxford University Press.

Clayton, Matthew, and Williams, Andrew (eds) (2002), *The Ideal of Equality*, Basingstoke: Palgrave, now Palgrave Macmillan.

Coady, C. A. J. (1991), 'Politics and the Problem of Dirty Hands', in Peter Singer (ed.), *A Companion to Ethics*, Cambridge: Blackwell, 422–30.

Cohen, G. A. (1978), *Karl Marx's Theory of History: A Defence*, Princeton: Princeton University Press.

Cohen, G. A. (1982), 'Functional Explanation, Consequence Explanation, and Marxism', *Inquiry* 25, 27–56.

Cohen, G. A. (1986), *Self-Ownership, Freedom and Equality*, Cambridge: Cambridge University Press.

Cohen, G. A. (1995), *Self-Ownership, Freedom and Equality*, Cambridge: Cambridge University Press.

Cohen, G. A. (2000), *If You're an Egalitarian, How Come You're So Rich?* Cambridge, MA: Harvard University Press.

Cohen, Joshua (1997), 'Deliberation and Democratic Legitimacy', in James Bohman (ed.), *Deliberative Democracy*, Cambridge, MA: MIT Press, 67–92.

Crisp, Roger, and Hooker, Brad (2000), *Well-Being and Morality: Essays in Honour of James Griffin*, Oxford: Oxford University Press.

Cullity, Garrett (1995), 'Moral Free Riding', *Philosophy and Public Affairs* 24, 3–34.

Daniels, Norman (1975), *Reading Rawls: Critical Studies on Rawls' 'Theory of Justice'*, New York: Basic Books.

De Wijze, Stephen (2004), 'Tragic-Remorse – the Anguish of Dirty Hands', *Ethical Theory and Moral Practice* 7 (5), 453–71.

Dent, Nicholas (2005), *Rousseau*, London: Routledge.

Drolet, Michael (2003), *The Postmodernism Reader*, London: Routledge.

Dworkin, Gerald (1988), *The Theory and Practice of Autonomy*, Cambridge: Cambridge University Press.

Dworkin, Ronald (1981a), 'What Is Equality? Part I: Equality of Welfare', *Philosophy and Public Affairs* 10, 185–246.

Dworkin, Ronald (1981b), 'What Is Equality? Part 2: Equality of Resources', *Philosophy and Public Affairs* 10, 283–345.

Eatwell, Roger (2003), *The Nature of Fascism*, London: Pimlico.

Edmonds, David (2006), *The Philosophy of Discrimination*, London: Routledge.

Elster, J. (1982), 'Marxism, Functionalism and Game Theory', *Theory and Society* 11, 453–82.

Elster, J. (1983), *Sour Grapes: Studies in the Subversion of Rationality*, Cambridge: Cambridge University Press.

Elster, J. (1985), *Making Sense of Marx*, Cambridge: Cambridge University Press.

Elster, J. (1997), 'The Market and the Forum: Three Varieties of Political Theory', in James Bohman (ed.), *Deliberative Democracy*, Cambridge, MA: MIT Press, 3–34.

Elster, J., and Moene, K. (1989), *Alternatives to Capitalism*, Cambridge: Cambridge University Press.

Etzioni, Amatai (1993), *The Spirit of Community Rights, Responsibilities and the Communitarian Agenda*, New York: Crown Publishers.

Finnis, John (1973), 'The Rights and Wrongs of Abortion: A Reply to Judith Thomson', *Philosophy and Public Affairs* 2, 117–45.

Finnis, John (1980), *Natural Law and Natural Rights*, Oxford: Clarendon Press.

Flikschuh, Katrin (2000), *Kant and Modern Political Philosophy*, Cambridge: Cambridge University Press.

Franco, Paul (2004), *Michael Oakeshott: An Introduction*, London: Yale University Press.

Frankfurt, Harry (1987), 'Equality as a Moral Ideal', *Ethics* 98, 21–43.

Gallie, W. B. (1956), 'Essentially Contested Concepts', *Proceedings of the Aristotelian Society* 56, 167–98.

Gauthier, David (1977), 'The Social Contract as Ideology', *Philosophy and Public Affairs* 6, 130–64.

Gauthier, David (1986), *Morals by Agreement*, New York: Clarendon Press.

Geras, Norman (1997), 'Solidarity in the Conversation of Humankind', *Res Publica* 3 (1), 105–14.

Geuss, Raymond (1981), *The Idea of a Critical Theory*, Cambridge: Cambridge University Press.

Gilligan, Carol (1982), *In a Different Voice: Psychological Theory and Women's Development*, London: Harvard University Press.

Goodin, Robert E. (1975), 'How to Determine Who Should Get What', *Ethics* 85, 310–21.

Grant, Robert D. (1990), *Oakeshott*, London: Claridge Press.

Gray, John (1983), *Mill on Liberty: A Defence*, London: Routledge and Kegan Paul.

Gray, John (1986), *Hayek on Liberty*, Oxford: Blackwell.

Gutting, Gary (2005), *The Cambridge Companion to Foucault*, Cambridge: Cambridge University Press.

Habermas, Jürgen (1986), *The Theory of Communicative Action*, Cambridge: Polity.

Habermas, Jürgen (1996), *Between Facts and Norms*, Cambridge: Polity.

Hamilton, Lawrence (2003), *The Political Philosophy of Needs*, Cambridge: Cambridge University Press.

Hampton, Jean (1986), *Hobbes and the Social Contract Tradition*, New York: Cambridge University Press.

Harrison, Ross (1983), *Bentham*, London: Routledge and Kegan Paul.

Hart, H. L. A. (1955), 'Are There Any Natural Rights?', *Philosophical Review* 64, 175–91.

Hayek, Friedrich August von (1944), *The Road to Serfdom*, London: Routledge.

Hayek, Friedrich August von (1988), *The Fatal Conceit: The Errors of Socialism*, London: Routledge.

Hegel, Georg Wilhelm Friedrich [1820] (1991), *Elements of the Philososphy of Right*, trans. H. B. Nesbit, Cambridge: Cambridge University Press.

Held, David (1996), *Models of Democracy*, Cambridge: Polity.

Hobbes, Thomas [1651] (1996), *Leviathan*, Cambridge: Cambridge University Press.

Honohan, Iseult (2002), *Civic Republicanism*, London: Routledge.

Hooker, Brad (2000), *Ideal Code, Real World: A Rule-Consequentialist Theory of Morality*, Oxford: Oxford University Press.

Horkheimer, Max, and Adorno, Theodor [1947] (2002), *Dialectic of Enlightenment*, Stanford, CA: Stanford University Press.

Horton, J. (1992), *Political Obligation*, Atlantic Highlands, NJ: Humanities Press.

Horton, John, and Mendus, Susan (1991), *John Locke: A Letter Concerning Toleration in Focus*, London: Routledge.

Horton, John, and Mendus, Susan (eds) (1994), *After Macintyre*, Cambridge: Polity.

Hursthouse, Rosalind (1987), *Beginning Lives*, London: Routledge.

Hursthouse, Rosalind (1991), 'Virtue Theory and Abortion', *Philosophy and Public Affairs* 20 (3), 223–46.

Hursthouse, Rosalind (1999), *On Virtue Ethics*, Oxford: Oxford University Press.

Huxley, Aldous (1932), *Brave New World*, London: Chatto and Windus.

Ignatieff, Michael (1998), *Isaiah Berlin*, New York: Random House.

Kant, Immanuel [1793] (1991), 'On the Common Saying "This may be true in theory, but it does not apply in practice"', trans. H. B. Nisbet, in H. Reiss (ed.), *Kant: Political Writings*, Cambridge: Cambridge University Press.

Keane, John (1995), *Tom Paine: A Political Life*, Boston, MA: Little Brown.

Kekes, John (1999), *A Case for Conservatism*, Cornell: Cornell University Press.

Kenny, Anthony (1980), *Aquinas*, Oxford: Oxford University Press.

Klosko, George (1992), *The Principle of Fairness and Politcal Obligation*, Lanham, MD: Roman & Littlefield.

Klosko, George (1994), 'Political Obligation and the Natural Duties of Justice', *Philosophy and Public Affairs* 23, 251–70.

Knowles, Dudley (1983), 'Hegel on Property and Personality', *Philosophical Quarterly* 33, 45–62.

Knowles, Dudley (2002), *Hegel and the Philosophy of Right*, London: Routledge.

Kolakowski, L. (2005), *Main Currents of Marxism*, New York: W. W. Norton.

Kymlicka, Will (1995), *Multi-Cultural Citizenship*, Oxford: Oxford University Press.

Lenin, Vladimir Ilyich ([1902] 1988), *What Is to Be Done?*, London: Penguin.

Locke, John [1689] (1988), *Two Treatises of Government*, Cambridge: Cambridge University Press.

Lukes, Steven (1987), *Marxism and Morality*, Oxford: Oxford University Press.

Lukes, Steven (2004), *Power*, 2nd edn, Basingstoke: Palgrave Macmillan.

MacCallum, Gerard (1967), 'Negative and Positive Freedom', *Philosophical Review* 76, 312–34.

Machiavelli, Niccolo [1513] (1988), *The Prince*, Cambridge: Cambridge University Press.

Macintyre, Alasdair (1981), *After Virtue: A Study in Moral Theory*, Notre Dame: University of Notre Dame Press.

Macintyre, Alasdair (1984), *Is Patriotism a Virtue?* The Lindley Lecture, Lawrence: Department of Philosophy, University of Kansas.

Macintyre, Alasdair (1988), *Whose Justice? Which Rationality?* Notre Dame: University of Notre Dame Press.

MacIntyre, Alasdair (1990), *Three Rival Versions of Moral Enquiry: Encyclopaedia, Genealogy, and Tradition*, Notre Dame: University of Notre Dame Press.

McKinnon, Catharine (1993), *Only Words*, Cambridge, MA: Harvard University Press.

Macpherson, Crawford Brough (1962), *The Political Theory of Possessive Individualism: Hobbes to Locke*, Oxford: Clarendon Press.

Macpherson, Crawford Brough (1980), *Burke*, Oxford: Oxford University Press.

Marx, Karl (1844), *Economic and Philosophical Manuscripts of 1844*, in Marx 1944.

Marx, Karl [1843–7] (1994), *Early Political Writings*, Cambridge: Cambridge University Press.

Marx, Karl [1847–83] (1996), *Later Political Writings*, Cambridge: Cambridge University Press.

Matravers, Matt (ed.) (1999), *Political Theory and Punishment*, Oxford: Hart.

Miller, David (1981), *Philosophy and Ideology in Hume's Political Thought*, Oxford: Oxford University Press.

Miller, David (1995), *On Nationality*, Oxford: Oxford University Press.

Miller, Fred D. (1995), *Nature, Justice, and Rights in Aristotle's Politics*, Oxford: Oxford University Press.

More, Thomas [1516] (1995), *Utopia*, Cambridge: Cambridge University Press.

Mulgan, R. G. (1977), *Aristotle's Political Theory: An Introduction for Students of Political Theory*, Oxford: Oxford University Press.

Naess, Arne (1989), *Ecology, Community and Lifestyle*, Cambridge: Cambridge University Press.

Nozick, Robert (1974), *Anarchy, State, and Utopia*, New York: Basic Books.

Nussbaum, Martha C. (ed.) (1999), *For Love of Country: Debating the Limits of Patriotism*, Boston, MA: Beacon Press.

Nussbaum, Martha C., and Sen, Amartya (1993), *The Quality of Life*, Oxford: Oxford University Press.

Okin, Susan Moller (1987), 'Justice and Gender', *Philosophy and Public Affairs* 16, 42–72.

Okin, Susan Moller (1991), *Justice, Gender and the Family*, New York: Basic Books.

Okin, Susan Moller (1999), *Is Multiculturalism Bad for Women?*, Princeton: Princeton University Press.

Ollman, Bertell (1971), *Alienation: Marx's Conception of Man in Capitalist Society*, London: Cambridge University Press.

O'Neill, Onora (1990), *Constructions of Reason: Explorations of Kant's Practical Philosophy*, Cambridge: Cambridge University Press.

Orwell, George (1949), *Nineteen Eighty-four*, London: Secker and Warburg.

Paine, Thomas (2000), *Political Writings*, Cambridge: Cambridge University Press.

Parekh, Bhikhu C. (1975), *The Concept of Socialism*, London: Croom Helm.

Parfit, Derek (1982), 'Future Generations: Further Problems', *Philosophy and Public Affairs* 11, 113–72.

Parfit, Derek (1997), 'Equality and Priority', *Ratio* 10 (3), 202–21.

Pateman, Carole (1988), *The Sexual Contract*, Stanford, CA: Stanford University Press.

Plamenatz, J. P. (1968), *Consent, Freedom and Political Obligation*, Oxford: Oxford University Press.

Plato [c.360 BCE] (2000), *The Republic*, Cambridge: Cambridge University Press.

Pogge, Thomas W. (1989), *Realizing Rawls*, Ithaca: Cornell University Press.

Pogge, Thomas W., and Kosch, Micelle (2007), *John Rawls: His Life and Theory of Justice*, Oxford: Oxford University Press.

Pojman, Louis P., and Mcleod, Owen (eds) (1999), *What Do We Deserve?*, Oxford: Oxford University Press.

Rawls, John (1971), *A Theory of Justice*, Cambridge, MA: Belknap.

Rawls, John (1993), *Political Liberalism*, New York: Columbia University Press.

Rawls, John (1999), *The Law of Peoples: With 'The Idea of Public Reason Revisited'*, Cambridge, MA: Harvard University Press.

Rawls, John, and Kelly, Erin (2001), *Justice As Fairness: A Restatement*, Cambridge, MA: Harvard University Press.

Raz, Joseph (1986), *The Morality of Freedom*, Oxford: Oxford University Press.

Raz, Joseph (ed.) (1990), *Authority*, Oxford: Blackwell.

Roemer, John E. (1985), 'Should Marxists Be Interested in Exploitation?', *Philosophy and Public Affairs* 14, 30–65.

Rorty, Richard (1979), *Philosophy and the Mirror of Nature*, Princeton: Princeton University Press.

Rorty, Richard (1989), *Contingency, Irony, and Solidarity*, New York: Cambridge University Press.

Rorty, Richard (1991), 'The Priority of Democracy to Philosophy', in *Reading Rorty*, Cambridge: Blackwell.

Rorty, Richard (1992), *The Linguistic Turn: Essays in Philosophical Method*, Chicago: University of Chicago Press.

Rorty, Richard (1999), *Philosophy and Social Hope*, Harmondsworth: Penguin.

Rosen, Frederick (1983), *Bentham and Representative Government*, Oxford: Oxford University Press.

Rosen, Michael (2000), 'On Voluntary Servitude and the Theory of Ideology', *Constellations* 7, 393–407.

Rousseau, Jean-Jacques [1762] (1997), *The Social Contract and Other Later Political Writings*, Cambridge: Cambridge University Press.

Ruben, David Hillel (1985), *The Metaphysics of the Social World*, London: Routledge and Kegan Paul.

Ryan, Alan (1990), *The Philosophy of John Stuart Mill (Second Edition)*, Atlantic Highlands: Humanities Press.

Sandel, Michael (1985), *Liberalism and the Limits of Justice*, Cambridge: Cambridge University Press.

Scanlon, Thomas (2000), *What We Owe to Each Other*, Cambridge, MA: Harvard University Press.

Scheffler, Samuel (ed.) (1988), *Consequentialism and Its Critics*, Oxford: Oxford University Press.

Scruton, Roger (1980), *The Meaning of Conservatism*, London: Macmillan.

Seglow, Jonathan (ed.) (2004), *The Ethics of Altruism*, London: Frank Cass.

Sen, Amartya (1970), 'The Impossibility of a Paretian Liberal', *Journal of Political Economy* 78, 152–7.

Sen, Amartya (1995), *Inequality Re-examined*, Oxford: Oxford University Press.

Simmons, A. John (1976), 'Tacit Consent and Political Obligation', *Philosophy and Public Affairs* 5, 274–91.

Simmons, A. John (1994), *The Lockean Theory of Rights*, Princeton: Princeton University Press.

Simon, Robert (1974), 'Preferential Hiring: A Reply to Judith Jarvis Thomson', *Philosophy and Public Affairs* 3, 312–20.

Singer, Peter (1995), *Animal Liberation*, London: Pimlico.

Skinner, Quentin (1978), *The Foundations of Modern Political Thought* 1, Cambridge: Cambridge University Press.

Skinner, Quentin (2001), *Machiavelli*, Oxford: Oxford University Press.

Smart, J. J. C., and Williams, Bernard (1973), *Utilitarianism: For and Against*, Cambridge: Cambridge University Press.

Steiner, Hillel (1994), *An Essay on Rights*, Oxford: Blackwell.

Swift, Adam (2001), *Political Philosophy*, London: Polity.

Swift, Adam, and Mulhall, Stephen (1992), *Liberals and Communitarians*, Oxford: Blackwell.

Taylor, Charles (1994), 'Can Liberalism Be Communitarian?', *Critical Review* 8 (2), 257–62.

Taylor, Charles (1975), *Hegel*, Cambridge: Cambridge University Press.

Taylor, Charles (1985), 'Atomism', in *Philosophy and the Human Sciences: Philosophical Papers*, Vol. 2, Cambridge: Cambridge University Press, 187–210.

Taylor, Charles (1989), 'Cross-Purposes: The Liberal-Communitarian Debate', in N. L. Rosenblum (ed.), *Liberalism and the Moral Life*, Cambridge, MA: Harvard University Press, 159–82.

Taylor, Charles (1995a), 'The Politics of Recognition', in A. Gutmann (ed.), *Multiculturalism*, Princeton: Princeton University Press, 25–85.

Taylor, Charles (1995b), 'What's Wrong with Negative Liberty', *Filosoficky Casopis*, 43 (5), 795–827.

Temkin, Larry S. (1986), 'Inequality', *Philosophy and Public Affairs* 15, 99–121.

Temkin, Larry S. (1993), *Inequality*, Oxford: Oxford University Press.

Temkin, Larry S. (2002), 'Equality, Priority, and the Levelling Down Objection', in M. Clayton (ed.), *The Ideal of Equality*, Basingstoke: Palgrave Macmillan.

Thomas Aquinas (2002), *Political Writings*, Cambridge: Cambridge University Press.

Thomson, Judith Jarvis (1971), 'A Defense of Abortion', *Philosophy and Public Affairs* 1, 47–66.

Thomson, Judith Jarvis (1990), *The Realm of Rights*, Cambridge, MA: Harvard University Press.

Thompson, Judith Jarvis, and Parent, William (1986), *Rights, Restitution, and Risk: Essays in Moral Theory*, Cambridge, MA: Harvard University Press.

Tooley, Michael (1972), 'Abortion and Infanticide', *Philosophy and Public Affairs* 2, 37–65.

Tully, James (1993), *An Approach to Political Philosophy: Locke in Contexts*, New York: Cambridge University Press.

Tully, James (ed.) (1989), *Meaning and Context: Quentin Skinner and His Critics*, Princeton: Princeton University Press.

Van Parijs, Philippe (1995), *Real Freedom for All*, Oxford: Oxford University Press.

Waldron, Jeremy (1981), 'A Right to Do Wrong', *Ethics* 92, 21–39.

Waldron, Jeremy (1987), 'Theoretical Foundations of Liberalism', *Philosophical Quarterly* 37, 127–50.

Waldron, Jeremy (1993), *Liberal Rights*, Cambridge: Cambridge University Press.

Waldron, Jeremy (ed.) (1985), *Theories of Rights*, Oxford: Oxford University Press.

Walzer, Michael (1977), *Just and Unjust Wars*, Harmondsworth: Penguin.

Walzer, Michael (1983a), *Spheres of Justice*, Oxford: Blackwell.

Walzer, Michael (1983b), *Spheres of Justice: A Defense of Pluralism and Equality*, New York: Basic Books.

Wenar, Leif (2005), 'The Nature of Rights', *Philosophy and Public Affairs* 33 (3), 223–53.

Wertheimer, A. (1987), *Coercion*, Princeton: Princeton University Press.

Wiggins, David (1987), *Needs, Values, Truth: Essays in the Philosophy of Value*, Oxford: Oxford University Press.

Williams, Bernard [1969] (2005), 'The Idea of Equality', in G. Hawthorn (ed.), *In the Beginning Was the Deed: Bernard Williams*, Princeton: Princeton University Press, 97–114.

Wolff, Jonathan (1991), *Robert Nozick: Property, Justice, and the Minimal State*, Stanford: Stanford University Press.

Wolff, Jonathan (2000), 'Political Obligation: A Pluralistic Approach', in M. Baghramian (ed.), *Pluralism: The Philosophy and Politics of Diversity*, London: Routledge, 176–96.

Wolff, Robert Paul (1970), *In Defense of Anarchism*, New York: Harper and Row.

Wollheim, Richard (1962), 'A Paradox in the Theory of Democracy', in Peter Laslett and W. G. Runciman (eds), *Philosophy, Politics and Society. 2nd Series: A Collection*, Oxford: Blackwell, 71–87.

Wollstonecraft, Mary [1792] (2004), *A Vindication of the Rights of Women*, London: Penguin.

Young, Iris Marion (1989), 'Polity and Group Difference: A Critique of the Ideal of Universal Citizenship', *Ethics* 99, 250–74.

Young, Iris Marion (1990), *Justice and the Politics of Difference*, Princeton: Princeton University Press.

Young, Iris Marion (2002), *Inclusion and Democracy*, Oxford: Oxford University Press.